C000067523

THE
PASSION
TRANSLATION

THE PASSIONATE LIFE BIBLE STUDY SERIES

12-LESSON STUDY GUIDE

THE BOOK OF
EPHESIANS

HEAVEN'S RICHES

BroadStreet
PUBLISHING

BroadStreet Publishing® Group, LLC
Savage, Minnesota, USA
BroadStreetPublishing.com

TPT: The Book of Ephesians: 12-Lesson Bible Study Guide
Copyright © 2021 BroadStreet Publishing Group

978-1-4245-6380-7 (softcover)
978-1-4245-6381-4 (e-book)

Stock or custom editions of BroadStreet Publishing titles may be purchased in bulk for educational, business, ministry, fundraising, or sales promotional use.
For information, please email orders@broadstreetpublishing.com.

General editor: Brian Simmons
Managing editor: William D. Watkins
Writer: Christy Phillippe

Cover and interior by Garborg Design Works | GarborgDesign.com

Printed in the United States of America

21 22 23 24 25 5 4 3 2 1

Contents

From God's Heart to Yours

"God is love," says the apostle John, and "Everyone who loves is fathered by God and experiences an intimate knowledge of him" (1 John 4:7). The life of a Christ-follower is, at its core, a life of love—God's love of us, our love of him, and our love of others and ourselves because of God's love for us.

And this divine love is reliable, trustworthy, unconditional, other-centered, majestic, forgiving, redemptive, patient, kind, and more precious than anything else we can ever receive or give. It characterizes each person of the Trinity—Father, Son, and Holy Spirit—and so is as unlimited as they are. They love one another with this eternal love, and they reach beyond themselves to us, created in their image with this love.

How do we know such incredible truths? Through the primary source of all else we know about the one God—his Word, the Bible. Of course, God reveals who he is through other sources as well, such as the natural world, miracles, our inner life, our relationships (especially with him), those who minister on his behalf, and those who proclaim him to us and others. But the fullest and most comprehensive revelation we have of God and from him is what he has given us in the thirty-nine books of the Hebrew Scriptures (the Old Testament) and the twenty-seven books of the Christian Scriptures (the New Testament). Together, these sixty-six books present a compelling and telling portrait of God and his dealings with us.

It is these Scriptures that *The Passionate Life Bible Study Series* is all about. Through these study guides, we—the editors and writers of this series—seek to provide you with a unique and welcoming opportunity to delve more deeply into God's precious Word, encountering there his loving heart for you and all the others he loves. God wants you to know him more deeply, to love him more devoutly, and to share his heart with others more frequently and freely. To accomplish this, we have based this study guide series on The Passion Translation of the Bible, which strives to "unlock the passion of [God's] heart." It is "a heart-level translation, from the passion of God's heart to the passion of your heart," created to "kindle in you a burning desire for him and his heart, while impacting the church for years to come."[1]

In each study guide, you will find an introduction to the Bible book it covers. There you will gain information about that Bible book's authorship, date of composition, first recipients, setting, purpose, central message, and key themes. Each lesson following the introduction will take a portion of that Bible book and walk you through it so you will learn its content better while experiencing and applying God's heart for your own life and encountering ways you can share his heart with others. Along the way, you will come across a number of features we have created that provide opportunities for more life application and growth in biblical understanding:

 ## Experience God's Heart

This feature focuses questions on personal application. It will help you live out God's Word, to bring the Bible into your world in fresh, exciting, and relevant ways.

 ## Share God's Heart

This feature will help you grow in your ability to share with other people what you learn and apply in a given lesson. It provides guidance on how the lesson relates to growing closer to others, to enriching your fellowship with others. It also points the way to enabling you to better listen to the stories of others so you can bridge the biblical story with their stories.

The Backstory

This feature provides ancient historical and cultural background that illuminates Bible passages and teachings. It deals with then-pertinent religious groups, communities, leaders, disputes, business trades, travel routes, customs, nations, political factions, ancient measurements and currency...in short, anything historical or cultural that will help you better understand what Scripture says and means. You may also find maps and charts that will help you reimagine these groups, places, and activities. Finally, in this feature you will find references to additional Bible texts that will further illuminate the Scripture you are studying.

 Word Wealth

This feature provides definitions and other illuminating information about key terms, names, and concepts, and how different ancient languages have influenced the biblical text. It also provides insight into the different literary forms in the Bible, such as prophecy, poetry, narrative history, parables, and letters, and how knowing the form of a text can help you better interpret and apply it. Finally, this feature highlights the most significant passages in a Bible book. You may be encouraged to memorize these verses or keep them before you in some way so you can actively hide God's Word in your heart.

 Digging Deeper

This feature explains the theological significance of a text or the controversial issues that arise and mentions resources you can use to help you arrive at your own conclusions. Another way to dig deeper into the Word is by looking into the life of a biblical character or another person from church history, showing how that man or woman incarnated a biblical truth or passage. For instance, Jonathan Edwards was well known for his missions work among native American Indians and for his intellectual prowess in articulating the Christian faith; Florence Nightingale for the reforms she brought about in healthcare; Irenaeus for his fight against heresy; Billy Graham for his work in evangelism; Moses for the strength God gave him to lead the Hebrews and receive and communicate the law; Deborah for her work as a judge in Israel. This feature introduces to you figures from the past who model what it looks like to experience God's heart and share his heart with others.

The Extra Mile

While The Passion Translation's notes are extensive, sometimes students of Scripture like to explore more on their own. In this feature, we provide you with opportunities to glean more information from a Bible dictionary, a Bible encyclopedia, a reliable Bible online tool, another ancient text, and the like. Here you will learn how you can go the extra mile on a Bible lesson. And not just in study either. Reflection, prayer, discussion, and applying a passage in new ways provide even more opportunities to go the extra mile. Here you will find questions to answer and applications to make that will require more time and energy from you—if and when you have them to give.

As you can see above, each of these features has a corresponding icon so you can quickly and easily identify them.

You will find other helps and guidance through the lessons of these study guides, including thoughtful questions, application suggestions, and spaces for you to record your own reflections, answers, and action steps. Of course, you can also write in your own journal, notebook, computer, or other resource, but we have provided you with space for your convenience.

Also, each lesson will direct you into the introductory material and numerous notes provided in The Passion Translation. There each Bible book contains a number of aids supplied to help you better grasp God's words and his incredible love, power, knowledge, plans, and so much more. We want you to get the most out of your Bible study, especially using it to draw you closer to the One who loves you most.

Finally, at the end of each lesson you'll find a section called "Talking It Out." This contains questions and exercises for application that you can share, answer, and apply with your spouse, a friend, a coworker, a Bible study group, or any other individuals or groups who would like to walk with you through this material. As Christians, we gather together to serve, study, worship, sing, evangelize, and a host of other activities. We grow together, not just on our own. This section will give you ample opportunities to engage others with the content of each lesson so you can work it out in community.

We offer all of this to support you in becoming an even more faithful and loving disciple of Jesus Christ. A disciple in the ancient world was a student of her teacher, a follower of his master. Students study and followers follow. Jesus' disciples are to sit at his feet and listen and learn and then do what he tells them and shows them to do. We have created *The Passionate Life Bible Study Series* to help you do what a disciple of Jesus is called to do.

So go.

Read God's words.

Hear what he has to say in them and through them.

Meditate on them.

Hide them in your heart.

Display their truths in your life.

Share their truths with others.

Let them ignite Jesus' passion and light in all you say and do.

Use them to help you fulfill what Jesus called his disciples to do: "'Now go in my authority and make disciples of all nations, baptizing them in the name of the Father, the Son, and the Holy Spirit. And teach them to faithfully follow all that I have commanded you. And never forget that I am with you every day, even to the completion of this age'" (Matthew 28:19–20).

And through all of this, let Jesus' love nourish your heart and allow that love to overflow into your relationships with others (John 15:9–13). For it was for love that Jesus came, served, died, rose from the dead, and ascended into heaven. This love he gives us. And this love he wants us to pass along to others.

Why I Love the Book of Ephesians

As a new believer, I began reading through the New Testament. I loved the Gospels, but when I got to the book of Ephesians, my heart jumped inside of my chest. It starts off with such a glory list of blessings that I could hardly take them in! In fact, reading Ephesians thrilled me so much, I think I underlined almost every verse. I committed this book to memory over forty-five years ago because I love it so much.

If you ever feel like you are neglected or you have to go without something you really want, read Ephesians. It is a nonstop list of blessings that you already possess. It easily divides itself in two parts: Chapters 1–3 could be titled "My Blessings." Chapters 4–6 could be named "My Calling." When you know how much God has blessed you, you will know how to use those blessings to encourage and build up others. That is your calling.

Two words stand out when I read Ephesians: "in Christ." Those words, or "in him" (Christ), are found over forty-five times in this book. To be "in Christ" is to have every spiritual blessing, including love, hope, and acceptance with the Father. I don't know of any other two words that encourage me more than "in Christ."

God has placed every believer into Christ, which means God now sees you as hidden in his Son. Your sins are not showing; he is. Your failures do not stick out when you come before the Father; rather, Christ shines through you. He sees you in the righteousness of Christ. To know that you are in Christ will secure your soul in the mercy and love of God. You are hidden in him, so now your true life is found in him.

Ephesians also touches so many of the important doctrines of our faith. It teaches us of the precious unity we have together in the family of God. It imprints us with the Holy Spirit, the engagement ring given to us the moment we believe. Yes, Ephesians reminds us that we, the bride of Christ, the body of Christ on earth, and the army of God, move forward fully clothed in his armor.

So many verses encourage my inner being when I read through this book. I know Ephesians will change your life.

Start your study today of this glorious book. Be sure to personalize every verse and take it into your heart as truth and life. May your journey through Ephesians bring you so close to God that you will see yourself clothed with Christ, tucked inside of his glory, and filled with his life!

Brian Simmons
General Editor

LESSON 1

The Apostle Paul and the Ephesian Church

The book of Ephesians is a very special book in the canon of Scripture. It is, in essence, the great constitution of the Christian faith, a powerful summation of the most basic principles of our foundational doctrines, followed by practical ways in which we are to live out this faith in our daily lives.

The church of Jesus Christ, his bride, is at the center of the letter to the Ephesians, with Christ himself situated at her head. Both Jews and gentiles have been brought into his body, and as the Holy Spirit fills the church with power, we—both individually and as a corporate body of believers—receive the calling to partner with Jesus in bringing about God's will in the earth. What a joy and a privilege we have been given!

> What an exciting letter Paul has written to us! Ephesians is full of life and its words reach higher in Christian thought than any letter in our New Testament. Full of living revelation, it simply drips with the anointing of the Holy Spirit. Where most of Paul's letters are addressed to churches facing specific issues dealing with belief and

practice, this isn't the case with Ephesians. There is a more general, theologically reflective tone to this letter that is meant to ground, shape, and challenge believers (mainly gentile) in their faith.[2]

Authorship

This letter to the church in Ephesus was written by the apostle Paul (Ephesians 1:1), arguably the greatest missionary-theologian of the early church. Paul was not one of Jesus' original twelve disciples, and he never even met the Lord during Jesus' earthly life—although he had an encounter with the resurrected and ascended Savior that changed his life forever (see 1 Corinthians 15:8–9; Galatians 1:1, 11–24).

Paul's great mission in life was to take the glorious gospel of Jesus to Jews and gentiles, and this he did throughout much of the Roman Empire to the east, north, and west of the Mediterranean Sea. For his efforts, he faced great persecution and other kinds of hardship (2 Corinthians 11:23–28). His letter to the Ephesians was composed around 60 CE, and Paul wrote it from a prison cell in Rome where he had been placed in chains for his passionate witness of Christ (Ephesians 6:20).

- *Most of us have never been imprisoned for our Christian testimony, but have you ever been persecuted (even in a small way) for your witness of Jesus and what he has done in your life? How challenging was the situation for you? How did it affect your relationship with the Lord? Did your witness of Christ grow weaker or stronger as a result of these difficulties?*

Recipients of the Letter

Paul personally knew many of the believers in the church at Ephesus. The city of Ephesus was located in Asia Minor, and the church there was a flagship of sorts to the other Christian communities in the area. Not only had Paul personally planted the church in Ephesus, but he also spent three years there, working to build the church and help it to flourish. Even after he left, the Ephesian believers were still dear to his heart, and he eventually sent his young protégé and mentor, Timothy, to be their pastor. Unlike the recipients of Paul's other letters, the Ephesian church was not experiencing any specific problems that needed to be addressed or that would prompt a letter from the apostle. Instead, Paul wrote this letter to his dear friends in Ephesus simply to encourage them in the faith and continue to teach them key truths of what it means to be in Christ and to live in Christ.

- *Read Acts 19:1–20:1, 13–38. What do these verses tell you about Paul's relationship with the believers in the church at Ephesus?*

- *What light does Acts 20:31 specifically shed on Paul's passionate desire and hope for the Ephesian church?*

- *Have you ever had a pastor pour his or her blessing and ministry into your own life in this way? What changes, if any, did it make in your life and in your relationship with God? If you haven't experienced this, what impact do you think it would have on you if you did?*

The Roman City of Ephesus

In the first century CE, what we know today as the nation of Turkey was actually part of the Roman Empire—and the city of Ephesus was located there, in one of the Empire's longer-established and more stable provinces, situated on the northeastern coast of the Mediterranean Sea.

The diverse people in the Roman Empire lived together under the *Pax Romana*, the peace of Rome. The empire's large military, extensive political administration, religious tolerance (at least for the most part), and application of civil law all worked together to achieve and maintain the peace and protection of the empire. The political leadership included an emperor, a senate, an assembly, and a host of lesser officials, including magistrates, governors, and even occasional client kings.[3]

The capital city, Rome, where Paul was imprisoned, was the home of the emperor, the senate, the assembly, and a population of about one million, consisting of at least forty thousand Jews, two hundred thousand poor men (so with wives and children, the number was greater), and even more slaves.[4]

Throughout the empire, the wealthy were quite rich, and a middle class thrived. Historian W. G. Hardy details "the immense volume of trade and the great prosperity which obtained in the

Roman empire in the first two centuries...The luxury was equal to anything the world has seen since."[5]

In the midst of this vast Roman Empire, the urban center of Ephesus flourished. The peace and stability its people experienced in one of the more-established Roman provinces allowed for a greater influx of trade and commerce, and so the residents of Ephesus enjoyed an even greater degree of prosperity than did many other provinces in the empire. Luxurious residences lined wide, manicured streets, and the markets were filled with vast and various goods from the far reaches of the Roman Empire.

In the center of Ephesus arose the great temple to the goddess Artemis—one of the Seven Wonders of the Ancient World and four times the size of the Parthenon. According to New Testament scholar F. F. Bruce, this temple "was supported by 127 columns, each of them sixty feet high, and it was adorned by some of the greatest sculptors of the age."[6] The huge structure "measured 370 feet by 180 feet and was located on an enormous platform."[7] Bible scholar E. M. Blaiklock adds that "the temple was the core of Ephesus' commercial prosperity. Around the great shrine, to which worshipers and tourists poured from far and near, tradesmen and hucksters found a living, supplying visitors with food and lodging, dedicatory offerings, and...silver souvenir models of the shrine...The temple was also a treasury and bank, in which private individuals, kings, and cities made deposits."[8]

Ephesus also boasted "a vast open-air auditorium" that "could seat 24,000 people." The city's civic assembly regularly met in this theater, and it was here that the city's populace "staged a two-hour demonstration in honour of 'Great Artemis of the Ephesians' and in opposition to Paul and his associates" (Acts 19:29–41).[9]

Politically, Ephesus was important because one of Rome's governors resided there. In fact, under Caesar Augustus (31 BCE–14 CE), Ephesus became "the first city of the Roman province of Asia."[10] In size, Ephesus was the second largest city in the Roman Empire, rivaled only by the city of Rome.[11]

When Paul had been a missionary for around seventeen years, he finally reached Ephesus and there founded a network of house churches, which eventually spread throughout the entire area. He spent three years in the city building up the body of believers there (during which time he wrote his letters to other churches, including those in Corinth and Galatia). After Paul later moved on to continue his missionary work, he was eventually imprisoned in the capital city of Rome, where he wrote his letter back to his beloved friends in Ephesus—as well as the new converts in the city, whom he had never personally met. These believers continued to keep the faith strong, and the lack of specific issues addressed in the letter to the Ephesians seems to indicate this was one of the healthier churches that the apostle Paul had established on his missionary journeys.

Key Themes

The apostle Paul stressed a number of key themes in his letter to the Ephesian believers. The first is one of the most powerful. Paul wanted them to know that before God rescued any of us through Jesus' passionate work on the cross, our situation was bleak indeed (Ephesians 2:1). There was nothing—nothing at all—we could do to save ourselves. But in his letter to the Ephesians, Paul shares this great and glorious news of the gospel: although we could never do enough on our own to earn God's favor, we are freely given this favor because of what Jesus has done. We are saved by grace through faith—a theme that runs through the book of Ephesians from start to finish.

Other important themes Paul makes clear in this book include the supremacy of God's power—over anything else in this world, including the power of the enemy. Paul also teaches the Ephesians various practical essentials for living out the gospel, including how to walk in unity, Christian conduct in the believer's relationships with other people—including in marriage, in the family, and between employers and employees—and our identity "in Christ," which is what enables us to truly live out this unity, love, and grace, as well as triumph over the enemy with God's power. Our position in Christ should impact every area of our lives.

- *Do any of these themes of the book of Ephesians speak to you more than the others? Which are you most passionate about exploring further? Why?*

- *How do your current relationships—in your marriage, with your family, at work—reflect your beliefs in God and the work Jesus is doing in your life? How might they need to change?*

EXPERIENCE GOD'S HEART

As you prepare to open up Paul's letter to the Ephesians, set aside some time now to come before God and be still. The Lord calls on us to "Surrender your anxiety. Be still and realize that I am God" (Psalm 46:10). The book of Ephesians is God's Word to his people, not just to those who lived two thousand years ago in ancient Rome, but also to us today. Settle your heart and mind. Don't rush through what God has to say. Be quiet for a while. Ready yourself for all he has to give you in this important and foundational book.

- *Write out a prayer asking God to speak to you through your study of the book of Ephesians. What are some questions you hope he will answer for you? How might you draw closer to him through this time of engagement with his Word?*

 SHARE GOD'S HEART

Paul wrote his letter to the Ephesians from a prison cell in Rome even while he was in chains (Ephesians 6:20). His devotion and passion for the cause of Christ and for encouraging his friends in the church at Ephesus were so great that not even his unjust circumstances could prevent him from sharing God's heart. Two thousand years later, believers still benefit from his extraordinary perseverance in the faith.

- *Share a time when persisting in your own Christian faith was especially challenging. What were the circumstances? What was the result when you persevered?*

- *What challenges are you facing today that might be discouraging you from wholeheartedly sharing God's love with those who need to know him?*

- *What specific steps can you take to overcome those challenges? Whose life might be affected as a result?*

Talking It Out

Since Christians grow in community, not just in solitude, every "Talking It Out" section contains questions you may want to discuss with another person or in a group. Here are the exercises for this lesson.

1. Being in Christ is a theme that Paul explores throughout his letter to the Ephesians. What images does this phrase bring up in your mind? In what ways would your day-to-day situation be different if you lived your life in Christ? How would your relationships with other people change? Your relationship with God?

2. The first three chapters of the book of Ephesians lay a foundation based on what Jesus has done for us, how great his love for us is, and what our relationship with God entails. The final three chapters outline how, as a result, we should then live out our Christian faith. Why do you think Paul organized this letter in such a way? How is right belief often followed by right actions?

3. The book of Ephesians emphasizes the fact that no matter how hard we try, we cannot change ourselves. Human strength or willpower will never be enough to transform our behavior. What we must undergo is a transformation that comes from the inside out, a result of the Holy Spirit's work in our lives. Have you ever tried to change a destructive behavior, an addiction, or a pattern of sin in your life through your own will or effort? How difficult was it? Did you ultimately succeed? What is a better motivation for change in our lives?

LESSON 2

Becoming God's Delightful Children

(1:1–14)

In *Reader's Digest*, the story was once told of a couple named Ruby and Arnie who tried for years—unsuccessfully—to have a baby of their own. Finally, they made the difficult decision to stop trying for a biological child and instead chose to adopt a baby boy. What a surprise it was when, shortly after the adoption was finalized, Ruby became pregnant, and she later gave birth to another baby boy, the couple's own biological child.

Years later, a neighbor came to visit Ruby, and as they sat and watched the two brothers playing in the yard, the neighbor asked Ruby which child was hers.

Ruby didn't hesitate. "Both of them," she said.

The neighbor, confused, tried to clarify her question. "I meant, which one of the boys is adopted?"

Again, without hesitation, Ruby answered, "I've forgotten."

Ruby so loved each of her boys that she no longer considered either of them adopted. They were just hers.[12]

Just like Ruby, God the Father has adopted us into his family as his own children, chosen by him and dearly loved. Because of Jesus, we receive all the benefits of this Father-child relationship, including God's grace, forgiveness, and transformative power, as well as the role he wants us to play in carrying out his purposes in this world.

In his letter to the Ephesians, Paul presents this great good news in the first few verses. As we delve into this treasured letter, give thanks to the Lord that Paul wasn't writing just to the Christians in Ephesus two thousand years ago—he was also writing to you!

Greetings from the Apostle Paul

The book of Ephesians opens with a greeting and an introduction by the writer, Paul (Ephesians 1:1–2). He identifies himself as an "apostle of Jesus." According to Bible scholar Lawrence Richards:

> The Greek word that is most commonly translated "apostle" is *apostolos*. The verb *apostellō* and a compound of it, *exapostellō*, as well as a synonym, *pempō*, are sometimes used with the same meaning: to send one on a mission as an envoy.
>
> At first these Greek words described the sending of a delegation of several representatives. Later the focus shifted, to emphasize the idea that an *apostolos* was the personal representative of the one sending him. Eventually *apostolos* came to be used in some Greek philosophical schools with a religious significance: the one sent spoke with divine authorization...
>
> Those [in the ancient world] familiar with the Greek translation of the OT [Old Testament] immediately identified the word with the OT concept of divinely authorized messengers sent by God and acting on his authority.[13]

This was Paul. He was God's authorized messenger. Paul was called by Jesus and sent on the mission of sharing God's love with the world. But Paul did not fulfill this mission out of a sense of obligation.

- *Read Ephesians 3:1. What does this verse say about Paul's motivation for his work for the Lord?*

- *What would you be willing to do because of your love for Jesus Christ? What lengths would you go to in order to share God's good news?*

Paul was writing to "all the devoted believers who have been made holy by being one with Jesus, the Anointed One" (1:2). Right off the bat, Paul is emphasizing that our holiness does not come from anything we could ever do on our own, but it comes from our union with and trust in Jesus, the Messiah, and the work he did for us on the cross. What wonderful news this is! Because of this truth, the second part of verse 2 now not only applies to the Ephesians but also to you and me as believers today in the twenty-first century. Read this verse and soak in the blessing that is meant for you, as one who has made Jesus your Savior and Lord:

> May God himself, the heavenly Father of our
> Lord Jesus Christ, release grace over you
> and impart total well-being into your lives.

- *What would it mean for you to receive God's grace and receive total well-being in your life today? What would change? What would stay the same?*

Becoming God's Child

Do you remember waiting to be chosen for a sports team, accepted on the cheerleading squad, or picked for a dodgeball team in an elementary school PE class? That excruciating feeling of wondering if your peers would find you worthy, if you had what it took to be part of the group—it was exhilarating if you were chosen but devastating if you weren't.

Paul was writing to the Ephesians to let them know the good news that God had, in fact, chosen them—and each of us can receive that same good news. Even better is the fact that we aren't chosen to merely be on a team. We are chosen to be members of God's own family, his sons and daughters, with all of the blessings, privileges, and responsibilities that relationship entails.

Elsewhere in Scripture, we learn that even if our own human mothers and fathers reject us, God takes us up and adopts us into his own family (Psalm 27:10). Knowing that God has chosen you, adopted you, and loves you with an unconditional love can make all the difference in your life. It can bring wholeness and healing where there has previously been rejection and disappointment.

- *Read Ephesians 1:3–5. The amazing "love gift" we have received from the Father contains every "spiritual blessing." According to Paul, this is the reason we should "celebrate him with all our hearts!" How have you "celebrated God" recently? What could you do to celebrate him and his blessings more regularly in your day-to-day life?*

- *How could you share this celebration with the other people in your circle of influence?*

- *What do you think it means to be "seen as holy in his [God's] eyes with an unstained innocence"?*

- *What "stains" do you still carry that Jesus' blood is meant to cover? Ask the Lord today for his forgiveness and grace so that you may stand before the Father as an innocent child in his presence.*

DIGGING DEEPER

In Ephesians 1:4–5, the concept of God's choosing, or *predestination*, is touched on by Paul. This has been a controversial subject for centuries among Christian scholars, with no single position finding greater acceptance over its competitors. Any discussion of this topic must include, even begin with, the Greek term used in the New Testament for "to predestine." This term is *proorizo*, and it occurs just six times in Scripture: Acts 4:28; Romans 8:29, 30; 1 Corinthians 2:7; and Ephesians 1:5, 11. The term means "to mark out ahead of time" or "to predetermine." Lawrence Richards provides a helpful explanation of the term's use:

In the NT [New Testament], *proorizo* is used with specific focus. That is, just what is predetermined is carefully identified. For example, Ac 4:28 asserts that the events associated with and culminating in Jesus' crucifixion were exactly what God's "power and will had decided beforehand should happen."

Ro 8:29 identifies those who love God as "predestined to be conformed to the likeness of his Son." The next verse adopts the divine viewpoint of timelessness. [It] sums up what to us is a process, but what to God is so certain that it can be spoken of as a completed whole. We who love God have been chosen, predestined, called, justified, and glorified, with the whole process encapsulated as a single timeless event.

According to 1 Co 2:7, God's plan to redeem human beings through Christ was something "destined for our glory before time began."

In Eph 1:5, Paul affirms that God, out of love for believers, "predestined us to be adopted as his sons through Jesus Christ, in accordance with his pleasure and will." In the same chapter he adds that "in him we were also chosen, having been predestined according to the plan of him who works out everything in conformity with the purpose of his will" (v. 11).

Thus, the NT use of "predestination" focuses on salvation. That whole wonderful process—including specifically Jesus' death, our adoption into God's family, and our transformation into Jesus' own likeness—is in view.

Strikingly, these passages do not relate God's plan and the human will. Other passages make it clear that the choice to reject or respond to Jesus is the responsibility of those who hear the gospel...

In some way, God sovereignly orders history so that the uncoerced choices of human beings harmonize with his plan. Another striking fact is that the verb *proorizo* is nowhere used in Scripture to state that some people are predestined by God to be lost. What is clear is that each individual's choice invariably coincides with God's foreknowledge and his sovereign will.[14]

In chapter 1 of Ephesians, Paul presents both sides of predestination: namely, that God predestined individuals to become members of his forever family in Christ and that when they heard the gospel, they believed by their own will (vv. 4, 12–13). In other words, God has chosen us in Christ, and we have chosen God through our faith in Christ. Exactly how these two sides of predestination go together remain a mystery and a matter of disagreement among Christian scholars.

For example, some scholars argue that God's sovereignty and omniscience have predetermined what we as individuals choose, including our choice of Christ. On this view, our exercise of faith or lack of faith are what God does in us, so the salvation plan, process, and results are completely God's work.

Other Christian theologians see Paul's words about God loving us, choosing us, ordaining us, and adopting us as God's sovereign plan for those of us who accept Christ by faith. And these scholars view faith as the means that God has established for us to receive the benefits of salvation and its fullness. These scholars point out Paul's emphasis that these benefits come through "our union with Jesus" (v. 5) and our being "wrapped into Christ" (v. 3).

In other words, God the Father has chosen (predetermined) Christ, his Son, to be the fullness of salvation for those who freely choose to believe in him. We are saved in the Father's Chosen One, Jesus Christ. Once we identify with him by faith, we are then chosen too.

These positions are just two of the many solutions that have been proposed and debated. And among them all, other essential issues come up, such as the meaning and reality of human freedom, the role the Holy Spirit plays in salvation, and exactly what God knows, how he knows, and whether his knowledge includes or excludes the possession and exercise of human freedom. We have provided in an endnote several sources that explore this long-standing mystery of divine predestination and human freedom.[15]

This is a mystery well worth exploring. While we as finite beings cannot fully comprehend the infinite God and his plans and ways (Isaiah 40:28; 44:6–8; 55:8–9), the more we know him, the more our awe of him grows, and the more we grasp how incredible it is that he loves us and has chosen to lavish us believers with "every spiritual blessing in the heavenly realm" (Ephesians 1:3). In that, we can rest, live, and turn our eyes toward heaven in praise and worship and wonder.

- *Have you ever pondered the mystery of predestination? What are your thoughts? What does it mean to you to know that God chose you?*

- *Read Ephesians 1:6. The same love that God has for Jesus, he also has for you! Write a prayer of gratitude and praise to your heavenly Father for showering you with this kind of amazing love.*

God's Plan for Your Life

Because of God's grace, we are not only chosen, forgiven, and adopted into his family, but we also receive an understanding of God's "secret desires"—his ultimate plan for our lives, and his long-range plan for the entire world, to take place when "the fulfillment of all the ages finally reaches its climax—when God makes all things new in all of heaven and earth through Jesus Christ" (Ephesians 1:10). God's ultimate plan for the world is redemption! So how does his plan for your own life play into this? The next verse gives us the answer: "Before we were even born, he gave us our destiny; that we would fulfill the plan of God who always accomplishes every purpose and plan in his heart" (v. 11).

- *How do you sense God calling you to participate in his grand purpose of redemption in the earth? Put another way, how do you think your own destiny plays into God's ultimate destiny for all of creation?*

 EXPERIENCE GOD'S HEART

The amazing truths of the first few verses of Ephesians demonstrate the blessings that Jesus has secured for us. Because of him, God has chosen and adopted us into his family and given us a part in God's ultimate destiny in the redemption of the entire world. But we still live in the tension of the already and the not yet. We still live in a fallen world, and not all of the promises of God have been fulfilled yet. But he has given us a down payment of sorts—one of the greatest gifts we could ever receive: the Holy Spirit. The Spirit comes to live within us, sealing us as belonging to the Father and enabling us to live out the destiny he has prepared for us.

> He [the Holy Spirit] is given to us like an engagement ring, as the first installment of what's coming! He is our hope-promise of a future inheritance which seals us until we have all of redemption's promises and experience complete freedom—all for the supreme glory and honor of God! (v. 14)

- *According to this passage, for what prospects has the Spirit been given to us?*

- *What have you personally already received and experienced related to what will come to you more fully in the future?*

- *Do you feel the tension of the "already" and "not yet" in the world within you and around you? What promises from God are you still waiting to be realized?*

- *Write a prayer to the Lord thanking him for the Holy Spirit and asking him to help you trust him more as you wait for the fulfillment of all of his plans to be realized.*

❤ SHARE GOD'S HEART

According to Ephesians 1:14, the ultimate result of the fulfillment of God's promises is "the supreme glory and honor of God!" Theologian Charles Hodge once wrote: "The design of redemption is to exhibit the grace of God in such a conspicuous manner as to fill all hearts with wonder and all lips with praise."[16] When the Holy Spirit is operating in our lives as the seal, or down payment, of these promises, God is honored and glorified. Other people will observe the difference he has made in our lives, which opens up new and exciting opportunities for us to share the love of God with them as well.

- *Has the fulfillment of any of God's promises in your life ever made a difference in the life of someone else? How was God glorified and honored in the situation?*

- *Who in your realm of influence needs to hear the "wonderful news of salvation" (v. 13) today? Ask the Holy Spirit, who lives inside of you, to create an opening for you to share your story with them.*

Talking It Out

1. Regarding the New Testament concept of adoption, which Paul wrote about in Ephesians 1:5–6, Bible scholar William Barclay once wrote: "The person who had been adopted had all the rights of a legitimate son in his new family and completely lost all rights in his old family. In the eyes of the law, he was a new person. So new was he that even all debts and obligations connected with his previous family were abolished as if they had never existed. That is

what Paul says that God has done for us."[17] Discuss what light these ideas about adoption can shed on your own relationship with your heavenly Father.

2. What does it mean that God's intended climax for his creation is to "make all things new in all of heaven and earth through Jesus Christ" (v. 10)? What needs to be "made new" in our world? In our nation? In the church? In your own life?

3. Reread Ephesians 1:7–8 and list as many blessings as you can that we have received as the result of being "joined to Christ." How has each of these blessings made an impact in your life?

LESSON 3

Paul's Prayer for *You*

(1:15–23)

What do you typically do when you are far away from the ones you love? Most of us try our best to communicate with those from whom we are separated, whether that occurs through social media, email, or handwritten letters sent by snail mail. And as believers, we also have the privilege of lifting up to the Lord in prayer those we love who are far from us.

This is a pattern that we can see over and over in Scripture. Jesus prayed for his followers in John 17. Paul prayed for the Christians in Colossae and in Philippi—and for his friends in the church at Ephesus in Ephesians 1:15–23. His passionate words echo down through the ages, for his prayer not only applies to the believers in the Ephesian church thousands of years ago but also to us today. Think of this as Paul's personal prayer for you.

- *As you read through the verses in this lesson, does anything stand out to you about the requests Paul makes for the followers of Jesus? What does he not ask for that are typical prayer requests made by believers today? What did he ask for that would be considered an "unusual" prayer request in our modern churches?*

- *How does Paul's prayer for believers here cover their past, their present, and their future?*

- *As you consider your own walk with God, construct a prayer to the Lord that encompasses your own past (how God has carried you through), your own present (what he is doing right now in your life), and your own future (what his promises are to you in which you are still trusting). Thank him for fulfilling all of his promises in your life!*

Your Reputation Precedes You

According to Ephesians 1:15, Paul had heard about the "strong faith" and the "tender love" of the members of the Ephesian church. Of course, he had lived among them for three years before he left, then appointing his mentor, Timothy, as their pastor to carry on his work. But since Paul had been in their midst, many new believers had been added to the congregation—people whom Paul never personally met. And yet, he knew of their love and faith. Whom they had become and what they were doing were extraordinary enough to have been relayed to Paul, even as he traveled throughout the known world and was eventually imprisoned for his own witness.

Well-known Bible teacher Joyce Meyer had this to say about Paul's words in Ephesians 1:15–16:

> Paul had heard about the love and faith of the Ephesian church. I hope that when people hear about us, they will also hear of our love for all people and our faith in the Lord Jesus Christ. Those are the best things to be known for. Have you ever thought about what you would like people to say about you after you are no longer living on Earth? Do you prefer that they say you were wealthy, the president of a major corporation, or perhaps a famous actress or singer? Or would you like them to say about you what Paul was hearing about the Ephesians? Let's remember to focus our lives on what is truly important, on the things that are eternal rather than the ones that are merely temporal.[18]

- *What do you hope people will remember about you after you are gone?*

- *How can you live your life today in such a way as to make that a future reality?*

The Blessing of God's Wisdom and Revelation

Essentially, Paul prays for three specific blessings to come to his readers. The first is found in verse 17: "I pray that the Father of glory, the God of our Lord Jesus Christ, would impart to you the riches of the Spirit of wisdom and the Spirit of revelation to know him through your deepening intimacy with him."

The first blessing Paul requested was for "riches"—but not in the sense that many of us would ask for riches. His prayer was that the Spirit of wisdom and revelation would empower them—not for personal benefits, such as greater wealth or success, but in order to know Christ better, to develop a deeper intimacy with him.

- *What do you typically think of first when you hear the word "riches"?*

- *How can knowing Jesus and growing in your relationship with him be a greater blessing than material wealth or success?*

The Blessing of Hope

Hope is necessary for each of us to survive in this world. Without hope, there wouldn't be much reason for us to get up each day. But if our hope is misplaced in someone or something that only disappoints, that false hope can be worse than no hope at all. In Paul's prayer for believers, he wrote: "I pray that the light of God will illuminate the eyes of your imagination, flooding you with light, until you experience the full revelation of the hope of his calling—that is, the wealth of God's glorious inheritances that he finds in us, his holy ones!" (v. 18). When we place our hope in what is true—his calling on our lives, the glorious inheritance he gives to us—then the path before us will become clear and full of light.

- *Read the front page of a newspaper or listen to an evening news broadcast. Do the news stories inspire hope within your heart? Why or why not?*

Now consider what you have read about or heard in the light of the hope that Paul prayed his readers would experience. Ask God to illuminate you and fill you with light as you ponder what you have read and the needs they raise. Pray for some of the individuals mentioned in the stories.

• *Did your perspective change at all? If so, how? If not, why not?*

# WORD WEALTH

In 1:19–20, Paul prayed that believers would "continually experience" the power of God working through them, in essence the same power that raised Jesus from the dead. There are four different Greek words that Paul uses in this passage:

• *Power:* "I pray that you will continually experience the immeasurable greatness of God's *power* made available to you through faith. Then your lives will be an advertisement of this immense *power* as it works through you" (v. 19). The word *power* used here is the Greek word *dunameos*, which means "inherent ability; ability to perform anything."[19] This often refers to the mighty power of God, which is limitless in scope.

• *Works:* "I pray that you will continually experience the immeasurable greatness of God's power made available to you through faith. Then your lives will be an advertisement of this immense power as it *works* through you" (v. 19). The word *works* used here is the Greek word *energeian*, which means "the effectual working of ability."[20] We get our English word *energy* from this Greek word. As you receive the *dunameos* power of God, you apply your own *energeian*, cooperating with God as he energizes you to effectively put his power to work in your life circumstances.

- *Mighty:* "This is the *mighty* power that was released when God raised Christ from the dead" (vv. 19–20). The word *mighty* used here is the Greek word *kratous*, which means "strength in relation to an end to be gained or dominion to be exercised."[21] The power of God has a purpose, a goal, a focus, an intended result.

- *Power:* "This is the mighty *power* that was released when God raised Christ from the dead" (vv. 19–20). The word *power* used here is not the Greek word *dunameos*, which was used earlier in the passage. Instead, Paul uses the term *ischuos*, which means "strength that a person has; power in possession, ability, or latent power; bodily or muscular strength."[22] This refers to the physical power released to Jesus when he rose from the dead.

- *Consider for a moment the amazing, creative, transformative power that was released into Jesus' battered and lifeless body in the tomb, enabling him to literally rise from the dead. And not just to his previous human form but with an entirely new, glorified body! Now consider your present life circumstances and challenges in light of what Paul says in verses 19–20. Do you tap into God's incredible power? It's already at work*

*within you, conforming you to Christ, transforming you
into the person God always wanted you to be. Ask God to
help you understand how you can cooperate with him to
live out his power in your everyday life. Then go about
in faith, trusting that his power will continue working
through you, enabling you to live life his way.*

Jesus above All

Jesus' preeminence over everything in creation is emphasized
at the end of this portion of Paul's prayer:

> God raised Christ from the dead and
> exalted him to the place of highest honor
> and supreme authority in the heavenly
> realm! And now he is exalted as first
> above every ruler, authority, government,
> and realm of power in existence! He is
> gloriously enthroned over every name that
> is ever praised, not only in this age, but in
> the age that is coming! (vv. 20–21).

Most Bible scholars believe that the rulers in authority Paul
was referring to in these verses were primarily demonic principalities and powers over which Jesus has ultimate control. In Paul's
day, demonic activity was common and the source of much fear,
and in the city of Ephesus, a thriving industry had arisen to try
to influence demonic activity through the occult. Astrologers and

wizards filled the Ephesian markets with trinkets, potions, and spells designed to ward off evil.

Paul's ministry in Ephesus had a profound impact on the occult business there. Luke tells us in Acts that during Paul's ministry years in Ephesus, "Large numbers of those who had been practicing magic took all of their books and scrolls of spells and incantations and publicly burned them. When the value of all the books and scrolls was calculated, it all came to several million dollars" (Acts 19:19).

New Testament scholar Clinton Arnold explains that in Paul's day, "Magic was based on the belief in supernatural powers which could be harnessed and used by appropriating the correct technique." Put another way, magic was a "method of manipulating supernatural powers to accomplish certain tasks with guaranteed results. Magicians would not seek the will of the deity in a matter, but would invoke the deity to do precisely as they stated." The gods and their assistants—spirits called angels and daimons— could be influenced to accomplish one's bidding as long as the magician correctly performed the magical formula or rite. Spirit beings allegedly populated such places as the heavenlies, the air, forests, rivers, seas, homes, animals, and the underworld. People in the ancient world feared them and used magic to call on some of them to provide protection from other spirits. People also believed that these powers ruled over them, determining their fate. And yet people would try to influence these powers to "compel the physical attraction of another person (aphrodisiacs), to gain favor and influence with people, to heal various kinds of illnesses... and to gain an appearance from a deity who could reveal special knowledge."[23]

People also struggled with the many human authorities over them in the ancient world, especially those found in government. And human authority figures could be as capricious and overwhelming as spirit powers.

Paul acknowledged all such powers, but he denied that their influence over human life was supreme. Someone had real and final control over all of them, and that someone was Jesus Christ! "Ephesians emphasizes the triumph and sovereignty of Christ over every power—known or unknown, real or imagined, present or future."[24] Christ is and always will be over "every ruler, authority, government, and realm of power in existence" (Ephesians 1:21). We need not live in fear of these entities. He who loves us, chose us, saved us, and adopted us is supreme over all other authorities and powers.

- *What does it mean to you to know that Jesus is Lord over all—including the political governments of our own nation and the nations of the world? Write a prayer thanking him for his power and control over this world's political and governmental structures and asking that his will for the nations of the earth to be done.*

- *What does it mean to you to know that Jesus is Lord over all—including the principalities and powers that serve our greatest enemy, the devil? Write a prayer thanking Jesus for his power and control over every evil plan of the enemy for your life and asking him that his will be fully accomplished in your life.*

 EXPERIENCE GOD'S HEART

Paul's description of the believers in his prayer in Ephesians 1 is a wonderful endorsement of their strong commitment to Jesus and to each other.

- *Read Ephesians 1:15–16 again and consider how you compare with the Ephesian believers in the areas of your faith, your love, and your service to other people. What do you think Paul would write in this passage if he were specifically writing to you?*

- *How could you improve in the areas you listed above?*

- *Take at least one item from your first list, along with the items you listed that could be improved, and ask the Holy Spirit to help you come up with a plan to implement that life change. Then put it into action.*

❤ SHARE GOD'S HEART

When God does amazing things in our lives, his hope and expectation is that we would demonstrate his mighty works—and the love he exudes—to those around us. Paul wrote that when we experience God's "immeasurable greatness" and his power is "made available" to us through faith, the incredible results will transform our very lives into "advertisements" of his great power and love as he works through us.

- *What, if any, advertising campaigns in recent years have affected you, either by bringing you greater awareness of a product or persuading you to actually purchase what the campaign advertised? Why did the ad or slogan have such an influence upon you?*

- *One of the great revelations in Ephesians 1 is that we ourselves—our very lives—are a continual advertisement for what God is doing in and through us. What does God's "advertisement" in your life say to those around you? How can you improve the impressions people have of God's love and power when they observe your behavior? Your reactions? Your walk with God?*

Talking It Out

1. Ephesians 1:15–23 contains many beautiful images and phrases, rich in meaning and focus. Consider choosing one of the following (or another of your choice) that has a significant meaning in your life and meditating on it for five to ten minutes a day for the next week. Jot down any thoughts that come to mind or anything God speaks to you through his Word: "deepening intimacy with him" (v. 17); "God illuminating the eyes of your imagination, flooding you with light" (v. 18); "the hope of his calling" (v. 18); "the immeasurable greatness of God's power" (v. 19)·

2. This passage of Scripture is a wonderful model prayer you can use to pray over yourself or others on a daily or weekly basis. Read the verses aloud and insert either your name or the name of the person for whom you are praying in place of the word "you" throughout. For example, *Since I first heard about Bill's strong faith in Jesus and his tender love toward all his devoted ones, my heart is always full and overflowing with thanks to God for Bill.* This is a great prayer to pray for loved ones when you are separated from them physically but remain close in heart, as Paul did with the Ephesian believers.

3. The prayer in Ephesians 1 is not the only recorded prayer of the apostle Paul in Scripture. Take the time to read 2 Thessalonians 1:3, 11–12. What did Paul pray for others in these verses? If Paul were specifically praying for you in this passage, in what ways would you hope to "live worthy of all that he has invited you to experience" (v. 11)? What would change in your life?

4. Reread Ephesians 1:7–8 and list as many blessings as you can that we have received as the result of being "joined to Christ." Do you recognize these blessings in your life? How has each one made an impact in your life?

LESSON 4

Made Completely New

(2:1–22)

Who doesn't like a story with a happy ending? In many books and movies, the worse things get for the hero or heroine, the sweeter the ending is when everything works out. Perhaps we love these stories so much because there is an element of truth to them. They reflect the plot of the Greatest Story Ever Told, and as Paul describes it in Ephesians 2, it couldn't have gotten much worse. The entire human race—including you and me— was doomed to depravity, lost and hopeless, sentenced to an eternity apart from God. But then the Savior came on the scene, the One whom God had promised right after the first humans sinned (Genesis 3:15). This Savior, Jesus the Christ, offered himself in our place of judgment on the cross, and due to his sacrifice, death, and resurrection, we are moved from a situation that was indeed the *worst of the worst* to what is actually the *best of the best*: a life lived for Christ here on earth, filled with and empowered by his Holy Spirit, and a promised eternal life in heaven and then in the new heavens and earth with the triune God—Father, Son, and Spirit. There's much to the story yet to play out, but the incredible ending is known, at least to those of us who believe.

Life without Jesus

A "dead corpse"—that is the description Paul gives of all of us before we were saved and filled with the fullness of Christ (Ephesians 2:1). The defining characteristic of a corpse is that it is, well, dead. But death in Scripture does not mean nonexistent. As Bible scholar Henri Blocher explains:

> In the Bible, death is the reverse of life—it is not the reverse of existence. To die does not mean to cease to be, but in biblical terms it means 'cut off from the land of the living', henceforth unable to act, and to enter another condition...It is diminished existence, but nevertheless an existence. Proof of this is found in the representation of the departed as meeting in 'the house appointed for all living' (Jb. 30:23), who are 'joined to their fathers' and who greet and speak to one another (Is. 14; Ezk. 32)...
>
> If dying were ceasing to be, nothing more could be said about it beyond that simple statement; but since dying is still existing, other changes in existence will, by extension, be able to bear the name of 'death'.[25]

So the corpse condition of those outside of Christ does not mean they are unable to breath, work, love, hate, or do anything else in this world. It does, however, mean that they are cut off from the Source of life, separated from God. Human "sins and offenses" have brought about this death state (Ephesians 2:1). And this condition affects everything they think, feel, say, and do. They live a life that's not as it should be. Everything is damaged because they are damaged. Their relationships with others, their relationship with themselves, their work and play, their ideas and their execution of those ideas, their moral choices...all of their life is marred by death. This is not the way human beings were created to live.

- *What have you seen sin kill, corrupt, or damage—either in your own pre-salvation experience or in the lives of others?*

- *How do you tend to think of the people you know who do not have Jesus in their lives—as "unfulfilled," "not meeting their true purpose," or "missing out"? Or do you think of them as cut off from God, dead in their sinful condition? How would changing your view affect how you relate to them and your motivation to share the love of God with them?*

Paul ties our lost, dead state—the state of every human being outside of Christ's salvation—to the "religions, customs, and values of this world," ultimately influenced by the enemy, Satan himself, the "dark ruler of the earthly realm" (Ephesians 2:2).

- *The Christians in Ephesus lived in the midst of a pagan society. These pagans followed a number of practices to remove their guilt and transgressions—paying a monetary fine, animal sacrifices, abstaining from food or sex, or even self-maiming. Today, our religious practices may differ, but the attempt to deal with guilt and find forgiveness remains the same. What have you seen modern people do to try to alleviate the guilt they suffer from?*

• *How did you deal with this problem before you came to Christ?*

• *How can accepting the grace of God free us from such rituals and obligations?*

DIGGING DEEPER

Many Bible scholars agree that the three primary influences that entice human beings to sin include the world, the flesh, and the devil. In other words, our three greatest enemies include (1) the greater culture that surrounds us and pulls us to conform, to follow "what everyone else is doing"; (2) our own sinful condition, with our human passions and desires misdirected and often out of control; and (3) Satan and other demons who strive to tempt us away from obedience to God. All three of these enemies work against us to pull us toward destruction.

- *Which do you personally struggle with more: the world (e.g., giving in to peer pressure, seeking fame or power), the flesh (e.g., succumbing to lusts for sex, food, alcohol, or drugs), or satanic temptations (e.g., to worry, fear, steal, lie, cheat, or live more for self than others)?*

- *Describe how you deal with these sorts of temptations.*

- *Read Ephesians 2:4–6. How do these verses offer hope during times of temptation? How can you practically incorporate them into your spiritual walk this week?*

 WORD WEALTH

One of the best-known verses in the Bible is found in Ephesians 2:8. This is a *key verse* in Paul's letter to the Ephesians and in the New Testament.

> For it was only through this wonderful
> grace that we believed in him. Nothing
> we did could ever earn this salvation,
> for it was the gracious gift from God that
> brought us to Christ!

- *Have you ever memorized or studied this verse in another translation? If so, what impact has it had on you? If this is the first time you have encountered this verse, what does it say to you about God's gift of salvation?*

- *What kinds of things do people do to try to earn salvation? What kinds of things have you done?*

- *Why do such attempts fail, and what are the signs of their failure?*

Everything Is New!

In Ephesians 2:11–13, Paul was primarily addressing gentile (non-Jewish) believers. Read his words and imagine that Paul wrote them specifically to you. There was a time when all of us were outside of God's fold, "foreigners" to his ways, no matter where or to whom we were born and no matter our religious heritage, even if we grew up in the church.

- *How does the idea of being "delightfully close" to God make you feel? Apprehensive? Excited? Nervous? Contented? Why do you feel this way?*

- *What things were made new when you accepted Jesus into your life as Savior and Lord? What changed immediately? What took some time to change? What is still in the process of changing in your life?*

Peace with God

One of Jesus' most powerful titles is the Prince of Peace. Through him and his sacrifice on the cross, he has not only purchased our ability to have peace with God the Father through the forgiveness of our sins, but he has also brought peace between believers. According to Ephesians 2:15, even "ethnic hatred has been dissolved" as we all stand as equals before the Lord. We are all sinners, saved by his grace, and through him we are all now "one new race of humanity." What a life-changing message our world needs to hear!

- *As you look around at the conflicts between nations, ethnic groups, and even different ethnic groups in your own country, how have you seen people trying to "make peace" with each other absent the working of God or the presence of the Holy Spirit?*

- *What is the true answer to these kinds of conflicts?*

- *How can you personally and as a part of the larger body of Christ become a part of this "true answer" and make a difference in the world around you?*

🜲 EXPERIENCE GOD'S HEART

Paul uses a common phrase to describe the reconciliation we experience when we come back to the Father through the sacrifice of Jesus: "Two have now become one" (2:16). And this unity brings about our restoration to God and to one another in Christ.

- *Where do we hear the phrase "Two have now become one" most commonly?*

- *In what ways is your relationship with God similar to a marriage relationship? How is it different?*

- *How is your relationship with other members of the body of Christ like a marriage relationship? In what ways is it different?*

- *Paul writes of the transformation each of us goes through as we progress in our walk with Jesus. How do you view yourself as part of an "entire building…under construction" (v. 21)? What is God still working out in you?*

- *According to verse 22, God does this construction work "through the power of the Holy Spirit living in you!" How has the Holy Spirit made the difference in transforming you more into the character of Christ? How can you rely on the Holy Spirit more in this area?*

SHARE GOD'S HEART

Read these beautiful words written by Paul in 2:10:

> We have become his poetry, a re-created people that will fulfill the destiny he has given each of us, for we are joined to Jesus, the Anointed One. Even before we were born, God planned in advance our destiny and the good works we would do to fulfill it!

- *This verse, along with the words of Psalm 139, tell of the great love and care the Father had when he planned your life—before you were ever even born! Read Psalm 139 in light of what Paul says in Ephesians 2:10. What thoughts does your comparison bring to your mind?*

- *How have you seen God's plan work out in your life?*

- *Poetry is one of the greatest forms of communication in the English language. It is passionate, emotional, and conveys the thoughts and feelings of the author in ways that no other type of writing can. To be "God's poetry" implies that he writes, through our very lives, the love messages he hopes to communicate to us and the people around us. As your God-given destiny has unfolded, how have you been able to be God's poetry to those who can "read" your life?*

- *What is one way this week you can share God's love and passion for other people, allowing him to write his poetry through you?*

Talking It Out

1. Ephesians 2:14 speaks of Christ breaking down "every wall of prejudice that separated us." In the time of Jesus and Paul, the literal barrier of separation between the people and a holy God was the veil that separated the Holy of Holies in the Jewish temple. This veil not only was an indication of the barrier between the Jews and God but also demonstrated the barrier between Jews and gentiles, as gentiles had to remain in the outer courts of the temple. Jesus' death resulted in this veil being torn in two from top to bottom (Matthew 27:51). How did the removal of this barrier change things for the Ephesians' relationship with God and with other Christian believers? How does it affect your own relationships with other believers—regardless of gender, ethnicity, social status, wealth, and so on?

2. What tumultuous or stressful situation is facing you today and stealing your peace? Jesus not only gives us peace; *he* is our Peace! How can this become a reality in your current circumstances? What changes come about from having Jesus—the Prince of Peace—working in your life?

3. Ephesians 2:11–12 refers to the Jewish "covenants and laws" and the "prophetic promises of the Messiah" that are present in the Old Testament. Are you familiar with any of these? If so, which ones? Have any of the Old Testament prophecies fulfilled in Jesus bolstered your faith? If so, in what ways?

LESSON 5

The Divine Mystery

(3:1–13)

Mysteries have long been intriguing to people. Who doesn't love to curl up by the fire on a winter's day with a good who-do-ne-it novel? Secrets and mysteries are even more fun when you know something good is about to happen. Think of a child's excitement over all of the wrapped presents under the tree on Christmas morning or the fun you can have planning a surprise birthday party for a friend.

God loves secrets too—not the bad kind of secret, like a hidden sin or something you are ashamed of sharing with others. But God loves to surprise his children with good gifts. And one of the greatest gifts ever is the salvation that Jesus has made possible for *all* of us—whether we were born as a member of his chosen people or not. Your ethnicity, your social standing, even your past behavior—none of it matters where God's love for you is concerned. That's the greatest mystery of all—the secret Paul can't wait to share!

A Prisoner of the Lord

Paul wrote this letter to his "beloved friends," the Ephesians, from a prison cell in Rome, but in the first verse of chapter 3, he refs to himself as a prisoner of Jesus Christ for the sake of those to whom he is writing.

- *From viewing himself as a prisoner of Rome to being a prisoner of Christ's, what change would Paul's perspective have made in his attitude while in prison? How might this perspective have affected his message to the Ephesians?*

- *How does reminding yourself of the truth that Jesus is Lord of your own circumstances change your own perspective? In what life situations do you need to remind yourself of this truth more often?*

The Secret Divine Mystery

Paul seems excited to share a new secret—a divine mystery—with his readers, one that had been "hidden for ages past until now, and kept a secret in the heart of God" (3:9) until the time of Paul's writing, after Jesus' life on earth had ended.

There had never been a generation that had received the detailed understanding of this glorious and divine mystery until then. God kept it a secret until Paul's generation, and he revealed it to Paul and then to the rest of his sacred apostles and prophets (vv. 3–5).

- *According to verse 6, what is this divine secret that Paul was so excited to share?*

This secret was revolutionary at the time of Paul. Until Jesus' life, death, and resurrection, the Jews considered themselves God's chosen people. And unless a person was born a Jew and followed the Jewish customs and religious laws, he or she was a gentile—outside of God's family and not a beneficiary of God's salvation or blessing. Jesus changed all of that. He opened the path back to God for *all* people—Jews and gentiles, men and women, anyone who would accept him as Savior and Lord.

- *Have you ever felt excluded from God's family—perhaps before you were born again? Or have those who called themselves Christians ever rejected or looked down upon you? Tell the story.*

Thankfully, God never wants us to feel that way. Each of us has a place in his family and a role to play in his church. And we are not only united with each other in his body, the church, but we are also one with Jesus himself.

- *Write a prayer to God as your Father, thanking him for choosing you to join his forever family.*

- *What are the implications of being "one with the Anointed One" in your day-to-day life?*

- *How would an infusion of Jesus' power, wisdom, and grace change how you relate to the world around you?*

# DIGGING DEEPER

Saint Augustine, a bishop in the North African church in the fourth and fifth centuries, famously wrote: "In the Old Testament the New Testament is concealed; in the New Testament, the Old Testament is revealed."[26] Paul's new understanding of the "secret," that the gospel has been made available to gentiles as well as Jews, was promised throughout the Old Testament writings.

Look up and read the following verses and write the seeds of promise that God planted centuries before Jesus' arrival on the earth.

Genesis 18:18

Genesis 22:18

Genesis 28:3–4

Isaiah 11:10–12

Now consider the following New Testament verses and what they say about the inclusion of the gentiles in the New Testament church.

Acts 3:24–26

Romans 9:24–26

Galatians 3:8

- *How does God's love for all people—not just those of a certain ethnicity or nationality—affect your view of the world? Of those in your country or city who are different from you?*

 EXPERIENCE GOD'S HEART

Earlier in his life, Paul was one of the least likely persons to become a great witness for the gospel. Under his previous name, Saul, he persecuted the new Christian believers, even participating in the stoning of Stephen, the first Christian martyr who died for his faith. Paul never forgot the amazing grace that saved him when the Lord Jesus confronted him in a vision, revealed the good news of the gospel to him, and then sent him out as a missionary to share the amazing message with everyone he met. Paul wrote: "I have been made a messenger of this wonderful news by the gift of grace that works through me. Even though I am the least significant of his holy believers, this grace-gift was imparted when the manifestation of his power came upon me" (Ephesians 3:7).

- *Have you ever viewed yourself as less significant than other Christians you know, perhaps based on your past behavior or sins you committed before you met Jesus? What was that experience like?*

- *How has God helped you leave your past in the past?*

- *Despite Paul's previous life as a chief persecutor of the believers, God still had a wonderful destiny in mind for him—just as he has for you! How is God currently working out his plans for you in your life?*

🌑 SHARE GOD'S HEART

Paul underwent a great deal of suffering in his life for the sake of the gospel. (Read 1 Corinthians 4:9–13 and 2 Corinthians 11:24–29 for more background on what he experienced.) While writing the book of Ephesians, he was imprisoned in Rome for the crime of preaching the gospel of Jesus. It is good for us to stop every now and then and evaluate what we might be willing to suffer for the sake of Christ. Most of us cannot fathom being jailed, tortured, or killed just for preaching the good news or refusing to denounce the name of Jesus, although this does happen to many believers around the world even today. Those of us in Western cultures are hesitant to even give up even minor conveniences let alone suffer actual persecution for the Lord. May our "passion," like Paul's, be to "enlighten every person to the divine mystery" (Ephesians 3:9).

- *Read Ephesians 3:8. What is it that empowered Paul to preach the gospel? How can it empower you?*

- *Paul prayed that his friends—and we as believers today—would have boldness through Christ as we share our faith because of our "complete confidence in Christ's faithfulness" (vv. 11–12). How could a greater understanding and reliance on the faithfulness of Jesus produce more boldness in your witness?*

- *Who needs to hear a bold testimony of Jesus from you today? Whether it is through your actions, a decision you make, or the actual words you speak to that person, make a commitment to share with them your relationship with God this week in a way they can understand, however the Lord directs you.*

Talking It Out

1. According to Paul's writings in Ephesians and elsewhere in the New Testament, all barriers have been broken down through the work of Jesus Christ. These barriers include those of ethnicity, nationality, social standing, educational level, even political party. Many of us find it easy to relate to those people who are most like us, but what are you personally doing to reach out to those people who are different from you in these areas? What is your church doing to reach those groups who are less represented in its membership? How can you increase your participation in these efforts?

2. Ephesians 3:12 speaks of the boldness we can have as we approach the Father "as kings" and with "complete confidence" in the faithfulness of Christ. Do you have this kind of boldness when you approach God's throne room in prayer? If not, why not? What is holding you back? How would it affect your relationship with God to begin praying this way?

3. In Romans 11:33, the apostle Paul used the same word—
"riches"—as he used in Ephesians 3:8. Read and compare
his words in these two passages. What are the "riches of
God" he is referring to? How has your own life been blessed
with these riches? In what areas do you need to receive
more of them?

LESSON 6

Walking in Love and Holiness

(3:14–4:6)

The apostle Paul's love and concern for the Ephesians is demonstrated when he "kneels humbly in awe" before the Father and asks for certain blessings to be poured out on them. Unlike many believers in our modern time, Paul was not asking for material blessings or for a life free from trouble. Instead, he addressed "the perfect Father of every father and child in heaven and on the earth" for greater blessings—*spiritual* blessings—that would be truly life-changing for his friends (Ephesians 3:15). Let's take a look at several of the blessings that Paul prayed for the Ephesians—and for *you*—to receive.

Blessing #1: Supernatural Strength in Your Innermost Being

Read Ephesians 3:16.

Have you ever needed supernatural inner strength? Maybe it was during a time of turmoil or confusion in your life. Maybe it was following the death of a loved one. Maybe a divorce or the unexpected breakup of an important relationship caught you off guard. As people who are living in a fallen world, we will encounter situations that can leave us feeling weakened or in despair.

- *What situation(s) have caused you to doubt your own strength and turn to the Lord for help?*

Paul writes that the "unlimited riches of [the Father's] glory and favor" will cause supernatural strength to flood your spirit with "his divine might and explosive power." God's favor on our lives brings not just a small amount of strength—just enough to "get by"—but "explosive power"!

- *What difference would the infusion of such a level of inner strength make in your current circumstances?*

- *If you haven't asked God for the strength you need, do that now. He wants to give it to you even more than you want to receive it.*

Blessing #2: The Life of Christ Released in You

Read Ephesians 3:17.

The strength that Paul prays for, and that the Father offers to us, is not some mysterious feeling we will suddenly experience. It is Christ himself, living within us, his very life released inside of us that gives us the power to rise above our circumstances.

- *How is this life released (see the first part of verse 17)?*

- *How hard or easy is it for you to "constantly use your faith" during your day-to-day activities? In which activities is it easier for you to use your faith in God? In which activities is it more difficult?*

Consider the following activities. Which do you believe would help you to exercise your faith more? How could you implement these activities in your daily lifestyle?

Focused prayer time:

Scripture reading/memorization:

Fasting:

Charitable acts:

Giving of yourself (financially or otherwise):

Blessing #3: An Understanding of Jesus' Love

How deeply intimate and far-reaching is [Christ's] love! How enduring and inclusive it is! Endless love beyond measurement that transcends our understanding—this extravagant love pours into you until you are filled to overflowing with the fullness of God! (3:19)

• *How have you personally experienced the "astonishing love of Christ in all its dimensions"? In what ways did it "astonish" you?*

• *Consider the following adjectives that describe Jesus' love for you: "intimate"; "far-reaching"; "enduring"; "inclusive"; "endless"; "beyond measurement"; "transcend[ing] our understanding"; "extravagant." Which of these descriptions most speaks to your heart? Why that particular description?*

- When this extravagant love of Jesus is poured into your heart and life, it spills out, overflowing onto other people. How has an understanding of Christ's love and God's grace affected your relationships with family members? Friends? Coworkers?

- How could a greater understanding of this love change the way you relate to others?

- Paul prayed this prayer (vv. 16–19) for the Ephesian believers in the first century. Who might need you to pray this prayer for them today? Your children? Your spouse? A friend? A coworker? Your pastor? Commit to praying these words for that person or persons and share with them your commitment, if appropriate.

 WORD WEALTH

Paul's letter to the Ephesians reaches a pinnacle toward the end of chapter 3, where the apostle penned a passionate benediction to the prayer he has just prayed. He assures each of us that the blessings we have received are worked out in our lives through God's mighty power—and that he will move through us in miraculous power to accomplish more than we could ever imagine. In verse 20, Paul used an unusual word to describe this power. In the original language, the words "infinitely more" are actually a compound word in which Paul combined the words for "above," "out of," and "exceedingly" to create this word, which gives the idea that God's power at work in us goes so far beyond what we could ever imagine that it surpasses the bounds of human language.

- *If you look into your heart right now, what is your "greatest request," your "most unbelievable dream," your "wildest imagination"? Can you imagine God fulfilling those dreams? Can you imagine him exceeding them?*

👤 EXPERIENCE GOD'S HEART

Do you recall where Paul was when he wrote the beautiful words in these verses about God's love and power? He was imprisoned in Rome, but even so, he was not thinking about himself and his own distressing situation and suffering (v. 13). Instead, he prayed for the Ephesian believers and for you and me today. He focused his mind and spirit on God's strength and power and on Jesus' love instead of his circumstances.

> Paul's message to you is the same as it
> was to those in the Ephesian church. No
> matter what difficulties you face, no matter
> what you are enduring right this minute,
> no matter how bleak the future appears,
> no matter what your pain of body of soul,
> always look up. Focus on God through
> prayer and count your real blessings—
> the love of God and His power at work,
> strengthening you from the inside out.[27]

- *Go ahead. Count your blessings! How is God's power at work in your life? How are you receiving his strength today?*

- *Write a prayer, thanking God for these blessings and for the extraordinary gift of his love and grace.*

❤ SHARE GOD'S HEART

It's so simple to attend church, to put Christian bumper stickers on our vehicles, or to post a Scripture verse on social media. It's so much harder to live out our faith in our daily relationships. In Ephesians 4, Paul turns from writing about matters of doctrine and "right belief" to matters of practical ways to live out our faith. And he starts in areas that hit home for most of us, where the rubber meets the road in our Christian faith. In 4:1–6, he lists several behaviors that we should develop in our lives as we grow more and more "in Christ": humility, patience, gentleness, love, and peace and unity.

- *How do these five characteristics, when evident in our lives, demonstrate God's love and grace to other people?*

- *In which of these five areas do you need to grow more, allowing the fullness of God to transform your heart and your behavior? What would that change look like in your life?*

- *Who would be most affected by these changes in your attitude and life? How would this allow you to "share God's heart" in a greater way with these individuals?*

Talking It Out

1. Consider these words from Ephesians 3:17: "The resting place of [Christ's] love will become the very source and root of your life." What does this "resting place" look like in your life? How do the rest of your thoughts, attitudes, and behavior flow from that resting place of Jesus' love for you?

2. Paul describes the glorious praise that has arisen and will arise from believers in "every church" and in "every generation," "through time and eternity." What does it mean to be a part of this huge group of people who have praised God for thousands of years and who will praise him throughout eternity? How does the realization of your place in this body of believers encourage you in your faith?

3. The traits Paul mentions at the beginning of Ephesians 4—humility, patience, gentleness, love, and peace and unity—are considered in Galatians 5 to be fruit of the Holy Spirit's work in our lives. How were each of these traits demonstrated in the life and ministry of Jesus? How would a greater measure of these traits in the lives of believers today transform the church? Our nation? The world?

LESSON 7

Christ's Gifts to Us

(4:7–16)

Birthdays and Christmas are special times, marking special occasions, as we celebrate our loved ones and God's greatest gift to us—his Son, Jesus—by giving gifts to one another. While some of us dream of receiving luxurious presents of jewelry, a cruise vacation, or extravagant clothing, for most of us, those gifts that improve our daily lives make the most difference and carry the most meaning. Consider the friends and loved ones who have given you the best gifts throughout your life. They are usually the people who know you the best, who know what you need, who know what will bless your life in the most meaningful ways.

In Ephesians 4, Paul describes the special event of Jesus' glorious ascension to heaven, his ultimate victory over the enemies of sin and death, and how, as a result of this special occasion, he gave us his "grace-gifts"—gifts he knew would bless all believers. Because he knows us best, he can give us the greatest gifts!

The Triumphant Jesus

Our blessed Lord in His triumph over death
led captive him who had the power of
death up to that time, that He might deliver

those "who through fear of death were all
their lifetime subject to bondage" (Heb.
2:15). In other words, our mighty enemy
Satan is now a conquered foe. He has been
led captive at the chariot wheels of Christ,
and our Lord has now ascended as Man
and taken His place upon the throne of the
Majesty in the heavens, and there from His
exalted seat in glory He gives these gifts to
His church for its edification and blessing.[28]

When Jesus defeated Satan on the cross, he stripped the
enemy of his power—the power of sin and death. But Satan still
runs rampant in our world today, primarily because we allow him
to hold power in our lives. If we cower in fear, continue in disobedience, or simply remain unaware of the enemy's tactics, we
can thwart the work of Christ as he continues the "restoration and
fulfillment of all things" (Ephesians 4:10).

The impact of Eph. 4:8–10 is that Christ—
by His incarnation, death, resurrection, and
ascension—had become available to fill all
things ("fill the whole universe" [v. 9]). He is
able to give His people all that is needed to
fulfill their calling.[29]

When Jesus Christ ascended to heaven, he did so in power
and glory, and from there he has bestowed gifts—spoils of victory—to his people.

- *For most believers, it is easy to picture Jesus as he was
  during his life here on earth, ministering to people,
  healing and delivering the sick, even dying on the cross
  and rising from the dead. But many Christians neglect
  to focus on his ascension to heaven. How does picturing
  a ruling and reigning Jesus at the right hand of God the*

Father change your perspective of the Savior? How might encountering him as the conquering Lord of the universe change the way you pray? The way you read the Bible? How you witness to others?

The Grace-Gifts of Jesus

From his position in heaven, Jesus has generously poured out gifts to his people. Each one of us has received the gift of "supernatural grace" (v. 7).

• *What does the phrase "supernatural grace" mean to you?*

• *How can you take this gift, open it, and make use of it in your life today?*

In addition to the gift of grace that all believers receive, there are additional "grace-gifts" that the Lord has given to his church. He appoints some believers as apostles, some as prophets, some as evangelists, some as pastors, and others as teachers.

- *According to Ephesians 4:12, what is the purpose of these great gifts of Jesus to his bride, the church?*

- *According to verse 13, how long will these gifts of grace be in effect?*

 DIGGING DEEPER

In Ephesians 4, Paul describes the different ministry gifts that God has given to the church. While each of the five terms may sound similar, there are important differences:

Apostle: The term *apostle* means "one who is sent." It often refers to Jesus' twelve original apostles, including Paul, or to others who were sent out as messengers of the church.

Prophet: A prophet is an individual gifted by God to speak forth his divine revelations, whether that be "foretelling" (generally of future events) or "forthtelling" (of God's directives in a certain situation).

Evangelist: This term literally means "one who shares the good news." Philip, one of the first deacons chosen in the early church (Acts 6:1–6), was gifted with the calling of an evangelist (21:8).

Pastor: A pastor is the shepherd of a certain "flock" of believers, providing guidance and leadership in local church bodies.

Teacher: Those gifted in this way have the ability to explain Christian doctrine, Scripture, and their applications, and they are able to refute false teachings and erroneous challenges to the faith.

- *How do the ministries of apostles, prophets, evangelists, pastors, and teachers equip believers to "do their own works of ministry" (Ephesians 4:12)?*

- *How has a person with one of these giftings encouraged you in your own ministry and witness of Jesus?*

 EXPERIENCE GOD'S HEART

As we are influenced by the members of the church who have these gifts from God, the Holy Spirit works in us and through us to help us gain maturity in our faith. Paul describes what it will be like at that time when "our immaturity will end" (4:14):

> We will not be easily shaken by trouble,
> nor led astray by novel teachings or by
> the false doctrines of deceivers who teach
> clever lies. But instead we will remain
> strong and always sincere in our love as we
> express the truth (vv. 14–15).

- *Are you easily discouraged when trouble enters your life? As you mature in your faith, this should become less of a challenge for you, but it can still be easy to lose heart when we see the state of the world in which we live and the many difficulties that surround us. What progress have you made in trusting God with the trouble you see and experience?*

 SHARE GOD'S HEART

While most of us are *not* called to be an apostle, a prophet, an evangelist, a pastor, or a teacher in the church, that doesn't mean we are left out of receiving gifts from God. As Paul wrote:

> Every member has been given divine gifts to contribute to the growth of all; and as these gifts operate effectively throughout the whole body, we are built up and made perfect in love (v. 16).

- *Read Romans 12:4–8 and 1 Corinthians 12:4–11. What spiritual gifts do you possess? (Note: If you have never taken a spiritual gifts inventory, consider finding and taking one either through your church or online.)*

Joyce Meyer writes:

> Thousands upon thousands of people sit in church week after week watching someone ministering on a platform, but they leave and do nothing toward serving God in practical ways. They return the next week and the week after and may be proud of their regular church attendance, but they have the mistaken idea that someone else should do all the work of the ministry while they sit idly by and enjoy it. This is not at all what Paul teaches.[30]

• *How have you used those gifts to serve your local church and the larger body of Christ?*

• *How could you use your gifts in a greater way to bless other people—both believers and those who do not yet know Jesus? How will you help someone else know him better today?*

Talking It Out

1. What does it mean to be "strong" and "sincere in our love" as we "express the truth"? In what ways have you seen this principle put into practice? In what ways have you seen it *not* followed? What was the result?

2. What is the relationship between the grace-gifts that Jesus bestows on his church and the unity of believers?

3. The ultimate purpose of the divine gifts that we each receive is to cause the "whole body" to be "built up and made perfect in love" (Ephesians 4:16). How do you see others contributing to this "building up" and "perfection in love" in the church? How are you contributing to these things yourself?

LESSON 8

New Life in Jesus

(4:17–32)

Did your mother ever ask you the question, "If your friends jumped off a bridge, would you jump too?" That question speaks to the power of peer pressure and the importance of choosing carefully those with whom you spend time and whom you allow to have an influence on you. In Ephesians 4, the apostle Paul stresses the differences between those who are still living worldly lives and those who have been saved by grace and now are followers of Jesus.

Those who do not have a relationship with God do not behave as if they do. They don't know him, and they don't follow his ways. Their own minds and feelings are all they have to guide them in this world. In contrast, we have a relationship with God through Jesus, and we have his written Word and the Holy Spirit to guide us. His Spirit even lives inside of us and empowers us to live differently from those in the world. Thank God for this new life we have been called to live!

Sinners Behave Like...Sinners

Paul gives a stark description of people in the world who do not know the Lord. He calls their logic "corrupted" and their minds filled with "empty delusions." They have a "blinded under-standing" and a "deep-seated moral darkness" (4:17–19).

- *What does Paul say is the result of this type of sinful thinking?*

- *Paul implies that what we cultivate in our thoughts will eventually influence our behavior. What examples of this have you seen in the world? In your own life?*

- *In verse 17, the word Paul uses for "delusions" could also be translated "opinions."*[31] *How do opinions differ from the truth?*

- *How can a person who is overly committed to his or her opinions be easily led astray?*

- *Has this ever happened to you or someone you know? How was the situation resolved?*

Christ Followers Should Act like Christ

In contrast to the people in the world who do not know the Lord, those of us who do are to live differently. After his description of the "lewdness, impurity, and sexual obsession" to which unbelievers surrender their lives, Paul makes this dramatic statement: "This is not the way of life that Christ has unfolded within you" (v. 20).

- *Read verse 21. How have you personally "really experienced" Jesus and heard "his truth"?*

- *Here is an even more important question: How is the reality and teaching of Jesus seen in your life?*

Now Is the Time!

[Jesus] has taught you to let go of the lifestyle of the...old self-life, which was corrupted by sinful and deceitful desires that spring from delusions [those "opinions" we just considered]. Now it's time to be made new by every revelation that's been given to you. And to be transformed as you embrace the glorious Christ-within as your new life and live in union with him! (vv. 22–24)

- *In verse 24, Paul gives the secret to this life transformation: relying on the "Christ-within" and allowing God to re-create you in his own righteousness. Have you ever tried to rely on your own strength to live a life of obedience to God? How successful (or not) were you?*

- *Paul tells us that it's time—right now—to begin to live a changed, transformed life, one that marks you as different from the world, a follower of Jesus rather than of your own opinions. What in you needs to change today? What opinions do you have that need to be surrendered to the truth of God's Word?*

Live It Out

It's not enough to have right thinking, right beliefs, or right doctrine. We must also live out our relationship with Jesus—it must make a real and tangible difference in our lives. Paul mentions numerous areas in which the transformation brought about by Christ-within will change the way we live. Read what he says in verses 25–32. Now let's consider each of these areas and contrast the behavior of those who do not know God with what God calls us to do.

- **Dishonesty versus Truth:** *What attitudes does the world have regarding telling the truth? What is the standard of truth to which God calls his children, and how does it relate to the fact that "we all belong to one another" (v. 25)? Are you known as a person who "always speaks the truth"? If not, what changes can you make?*

- ***Unleashing Passionate Emotions versus Self-Control:*** *What do many believers practice regarding the expression of passionate emotions, such as anger, jealousy, revenge, and greed? In what ways can the enemy use our strong emotions against us? Where do you need to practice "emotional self-control" in your life?*

- ***Stealing from Others versus Earning an Honest Wage:*** *Are you completely honest in all of your financial dealings? How can a lack of trust in God's provision for us lead to the temptation to steal? Ask the Lord to make clear to you any areas in which you might be displeasing to him in this way and commit to make a change.*

- **Hateful Speech versus "Words of Grace":** *Controlling our words can be one of the most difficult challenges in life. Thankfully, the Holy Spirit is ready to help us when we give him control over what we say. What habits might there be in your speech that need to change? How can your words become a beautiful gift to encourage another person today?*

EXPERIENCE GOD'S HEART

Thankfully, we do not have to strive to change our behavior all on our own. God knows that we are merely human beings, that we are still imperfect in many ways. Our salvation does not depend on our good works nor on our ability to please him with our behavior. Even in our imperfections, we do not ever have to worry about losing our salvation because the Holy Spirit is the guarantee, the down payment, of the glorious future we have waiting for us in heaven: "The Holy Spirit of God has sealed you in Jesus Christ until you experience your full salvation. So never grieve the Spirit of God or take for granted his holy influence in your life" (v. 30).

- *How is it possible to take the Holy Spirit for granted?*

- *When believers commit sin, they grieve the Spirit of God. Have you ever been "grieved" about a break in a human relationship? How did you react? Do you think the Holy Spirit might experience the same reactions when we grieve him through our disobedience?*

- *God eagerly waits to forgive us even when we have not lived up to his standards. When we admit our mistakes and commit to following him and his ways, his Spirit works within us to change us from the inside out! How can you allow the influence of the Holy Spirit to direct you in your daily life this week?*

❤ SHARE GOD'S HEART

No matter what we say we believe, other people will be more convinced of our relationship with God by the things we do—the words we speak, the attitudes we carry, the actions we take.

How might each of the following actions demonstrate God's grace to someone who needs to know of his love? Choose at least one and commit to putting it into practice this week:

- *Taking the high road in an argument:*

- *Giving someone a well-deserved compliment:*

- *Paying it forward with an act of kindness:*

- *Writing a note of encouragement to someone who needs it:*

- *Graciously forgiving someone of an offense:*

Talking It Out

1. Paul states that when we allow anger or passionate emotions to control us rather than being controlled by the Holy Spirit, we are actually handing the devil an opportunity to manipulate us. Knowing this in advance, what strategies could you put into place in your life—before you experience strong feelings of anger or other passionate emotions—to prevent you from being manipulated by Satan?

2. Ephesians 4:32 seems to anticipate that there will be disagreements among believers or in the church. Have you ever experienced such a disagreement or conflict with another Christian? If so, did kindness and forgiveness lead to a reconciliation? Tell the story.

3. The contrast between life before Jesus and life after we experience him is made clear in these verses. We have been moved from darkness into light, from death into life! What are the greatest changes that took place in your own life since you accepted Jesus as Lord and Savior?

Living in God's Love, Light, and Wisdom

(5:1–20)

If you are a parent, you might have experienced the joy of watching your child try to imitate the things you do. Most kids pick up their parents' habits, expressions, and mannerisms—which can sometimes bring praise or sometimes bring embarrassment! God is the same way; he wants his children to imitate him, to spend time with him so that we pick up his ways and mannerisms. As his sons and daughters, we represent him to the world, so what we do matters. Let's take a look at how living in God's love, his light, and his wisdom can make a difference in not just our lives but also in the lives of the people we touch.

Live Out the Love of God

Continue to walk surrendered to the extravagant love of Christ, for he surrendered his life as a sacrifice for us. His great love for us was pleasing to God, like an aroma of adoration—a sweet healing fragrance. (Ephesians 5:2)

- Paul calls the love Jesus displayed when he died on the cross for our sins "extravagant," and there is perhaps no more fitting word. In what other ways has God demonstrated love in an "extravagant" way in your own life?

- Paul lists several sins that damage our witness of God's love to others. One of these is sexual immorality (5:3). Many people practice sexual sins while calling it "love." How are these declarations of love cheapened through lust and immorality? How does God's love differ from these human notions of love?

- *Another way to imitate the love of God is through our speech (v. 4). Speaking profanity or insulting others, especially when these patterns become a habit, are contrary to God's desires for us. We're to "guard our speech" against such verbal abuses and "worthless insults." Along with guarding our words, Paul gives us something else to do: worship! How can you foster an attitude of worship of God in your lifestyle? What would be the result in your relationships with other people?*

- *Paul tells us that greed is the "essence of idolatry" (v. 5). In what ways does idolatry promote greed in our hearts? What idols might you need to topple in your life so that you can better show the love of God to those around you?*

Light and Darkness

Paul could not have made clearer the contrast between how we are to live and how the world still operates. Praise God that we have been called out of the darkness and into his light! None of the behaviors that Paul has listed come naturally to us as human beings, but they are the "supernatural fruits of his light" as his Spirit works within us to change us from the inside out.

• *In 5:6–14, what differences are listed between those who live in light and those who are still in darkness? Instead of "associating with" (read: agreeing with and participating in sinful activities with) those who don't know Jesus, what are we to do?*

• *Who in your life needs a revelation of the truth? How can you share this with him or her today?*

The Wisdom of God

John Grisham, a bestselling novelist and Sunday school teacher, once shared a conversation he had that made clear to him God's wisdom about how to live his life:

One of my best friends in college died
when he was 25, just a few years after we

had finished Mississippi State University. I was in law school, and he called me one day and wanted to get together. So we had lunch, and he told me he had terminal cancer.

I couldn't believe it. I asked him, "What do you do when you realize that you are about to die?"

He said, "It's real simple. You get things right with God, and you spend as much time with those you love as you can. Then you settle up with everybody else." Then he said, "You know, really, you ought to live every day like you have only a few more days to live."

That left an impression on me.

Few things impart more wisdom than to face up to the fact that we will all die sooner or later.[32]

John Grisham's insights reflect what the apostle Paul wrote concerning how to live in God's wisdom: "Be very careful how you live, not being like those with no understanding, but live honorably with true wisdom, for we are living in evil times. Take full advantage of every day as you spend your life for his purposes" (5:16).

- *How would your life change if you began to live as if you only had a few days left? How would your relationships change?*

- *How can you "take full advantage of every day" that you have to further God's purposes in your life and in the world?*

 EXPERIENCE GOD'S HEART

Paul has laid out the differences between living our lives in darkness and living in the light of Jesus Christ.

- *Reflect on the life you led before you accepted Jesus as Savior and Lord. What was it like to live in the darkness?*

- *Now consider the difference Jesus has made in your life. How has living in his light changed things for you in your behavior, in your relationships, in your hope for the future?*

- *Write a prayer of thanks to God for bringing you out of the darkness and into his glorious light!*

❤ SHARE GOD'S HEART

When the electricity goes out in our homes, we typically grab a flashlight to be able to see what we are doing and avoid tripping over things. If we have more than one flashlight, we might pass them out to members of our family to help them to see in the darkness as well. In the world around us, Jesus has called us to be his light, the light of the world. Recall his words from Matthew 5:

> Your lives light up the world. For how can
> you hide a city that stands on a hilltop?
> And who would light a lamp and then hide
> it in an obscure place? Instead, it's placed
> where everyone in the house can benefit
> from its light. So don't hide your light! Let
> it shine brightly before others, so that your
> commendable works will shine as light
> upon them, and then they will give their
> praise to your Father in heaven. (vv. 14–16)

- *Paul has agreed with Jesus that we are to share God's light with those around us. He instructs in Ephesians 5:20: "Always give thanks to Father God for every person he brings into your life in the name of our Lord Jesus*

Christ." Name one person God has brought into your life with whom you can share his light. How will you share that light with them today?

Talking It Out

1. Read Ephesians 5:18–20. What characteristics do you see that describe someone who is filled with the Holy Spirit? Which of these characteristics could describe you and your Christian life? In which areas do you need to be more filled with the Spirit?

2. In these verses, Paul admonishes his readers to sing joyfully and to give praise through song. Music is a powerful way to connect with the Lord. What are some Christian songs or psalms that have been especially meaningful to you in your life? Why did they touch you so deeply?

3. How could filling your heart with the worship of God help you guard against the behaviors that Paul listed in 5:3–4?

LESSON 10

God's Design for Marriage

(5:21–33)

Marriage is not a manmade institution. God designed it and implemented it in the garden of Eden with Adam and Eve. Men and women, especially those who are married, are meant to complement each other, to work together as a team, and to rule over the rest of God's creation. That is still God's plan for marriages. But just as the ancient culture in Ephesus had downplayed and denigrated the idea of marriage, so, too, has our culture today. In Ephesians, Paul counters this by lifting up God's pattern for marriage and comparing this earthly relationship to the eternal relationship between Jesus and his bride, the church.

Mutual Support

What Paul says about marriage in this letter is one of several relationships he brings up as examples of what he means in 5:21.

- *Read 5:21, and then note here what this passage reveals about how members in the body of Christ are to relate to one another.*

Now read through 5:22–6:18. Below, identify each of the several relationships Paul mentions in his application of the mutual loving support believers are to show one another.

In 5:22–33, the relationship is:

In 6:1–4, the relationship is:

In 6:5–8, the relationship is:

In 6:9, the relationship is:

In 6:10–18, the relationship is:

- *Paul lists these relationships likely because the Ephesian church had issues in these areas. It's not an exhaustive list of relationships that the exhortation in 5:21 covers. What other relationships would call for us to be mutually and lovingly supportive?*

Wives and Devotion

In 5:22–33, Paul explains how wives and husbands should carry out supportive love toward one another. He begins with wives (22–24), but by far most of his attention is directed toward husbands (25–33).

- *How are wives supposed to relate to their husbands (v. 22)?*

- *Why should wives exhibit devotion (vv. 23–24)?*

- *What is the biblical concept of leadership (Luke 22:24–27)?*

- *Now consider Paul's description of love and record its essential characteristics (1 Corinthians 13:4–8).*

- *With the information you now have, how would you describe what a husband's leadership would look and feel like in marriage, assuming he was living it out in a Christlike way?*

DIGGING DEEPER

Paul's guidance to wives is not built on coercion but freedom. We come to God in Christ freely by an act of faith. God doesn't force us into his forever family. He seeks to persuade us, to woo us, to call us to himself out of the superabundance of his love. Likewise, when Paul explains how wives are to show their loving support of their husbands by devoting themselves to them as to the Lord, he envisions a marriage that far exceeds contractual or cultural expectations. He sees something richer and greater—a relationship bathed in mutual love, support, protection, respect, and devotion. He centers on devotion with wives, but as we'll see, this idea will spill over to what he says to husbands.

Christian theologian Manfred Brauch speaks to Paul's comments about wives and the voluntary submission (devotion) Paul wants them to embrace with their husbands:

> The submission of the wife to the husband is to be "as to the Lord." It is no longer to be the kind expected as a matter of course by cultural norms and forced upon women—who were seen as inferior to males in both Jewish and Gentile cultures. No, her submission is to be freely chosen, being there for her partner "as to the Lord," that is, as a disciple of the Lord, as one who followed in his servant footsteps, motivated by self-giving love. This kind of submission is not a reinforcement of the traditional norms; it is rather a fundamental challenge to them.[33]

So when Paul adds, "In the same way the church is devoted to Christ, let the wives be devoted to their husbands in everything" (Ephesians 5:24), we need to ask how the church gives itself to Christ. And the answer is freely, humbly, and lovingly. As Brauch explains:

What is the nature of the church's submission to Christ? It is freely assumed in humble response to his self-giving, sacrificial servanthood and his continuing empowering and nurturing presence. The church's submission to Christ has nothing to do with external control or coercion. For the life and ministry of Jesus demonstrates uncompromisingly his rejection of "power over others" as valid in the new creation which he is inaugurating (Lk 22:24–27). Christ stands in relation to the church, his bride, not as one who uses his power to control and demand, but rather to invite and serve.[34]

Husbands and Love

After addressing himself to wives, Paul turns to husbands.

• *How is a husband to relate to his wife (Ephesians 5:25)?*

• *Return to the notes you made on 1 Corinthians 13:4–8. Drawing from those, what would you say a husband's love should look and feel like?*

- *A husband is to love his wife "with the same tender devotion that Christ demonstrated to us, his bride"—the church (Ephesians 5:25). What expression of Christ's love does Paul then refer to (vv. 25–27)? What are the benefits Christ's sacrifice will achieve for the church?*

- *Although Paul doesn't list comparable benefits that a husband's love ought to bring to his wife, what do you think some of those benefits should be? What reasons would you supply from Scripture to support the items on your list?*

- *Paul then provides a supporting reason for husbands to love their wives. What is it, and why does Paul appeal to it (vv. 28–30)?*

- *In verse 33, Paul summarizes the counsel he's provided to husbands and wives. What does he say?*

- *Paul states that women should be tenderly devoted to their husbands as if they were expressing their devotion to the Lord. Husbands, on the other hand, are to love their wives as Christ loves his church—in other words, sacrificially and as an "obligation." How can you express this level of devotion and love to your own spouse (or to the Lord himself, if you are single) this week?*

The Great and Sacred Mystery of Marriage

Before Paul leaves the subject of marriage, he appeals to the pre-Fall creation norm for marriage first mentioned in Genesis 2:24: "A man is to leave his father and his mother and lovingly hold to his wife, since the two have become joined as one flesh. Marriage is the beautiful design of the Almighty, a great mystery of Christ and his church" (Ephesians 5:31–32).

Paul compares the relationship of husband and wife to the relationship between Christ and his church. Both relationships are divine designs, both are beautiful, both are mysteries, both involve union, and both are birthed and mature in love. In any comparison, there are also contrasts. Similarities always assume dissimilarities.

Under each column in the chart below, write down the comparisons and contrasts you see between the human marital relationship and the salvation-service relationship of Christ and the church. You'll find some entries already made that may help you in your reflections on the two relationships.

Relationship of Husband and Wife	Relationship of Christ and His Church
The union of one man and one woman in marriage	The union of Christ to as many humans of either gender who exercise faith in him
Requires trust in a fellow human being	Requires trust in God
Requires severance from one's parents	Requires repentance from one's sins

- *What conclusions about marriage would you make based on your list and Paul's teaching in Ephesians 5:22–33?*

- *How does Paul's analogy between human marriage and Christ's marriage to his church reflect your own marriage or the marriage of believers you might know?*

EXPERIENCE GOD'S HEART

Whether you are married or not, the Lord is ultimately the One to whom each of us should submit our lives, and in these verses in Ephesians, Paul describes various ways in which Christ Jesus has proven himself to be faithful to us.

- *Read Ephesians 5:25–27, 29. What does Jesus do for his church and for individual believers?*

- *How has the Lord shown himself to be trustworthy in your life?*

- *Do you consider yourself a "source of praise to him"? If yes, how so? If not, how could you become a source of praise for the Lord Jesus this next week?*

 SHARE GOD'S HEART

Married or single, each of us has a responsibility to share the love of God with those closest to us—as well as to represent his kingdom well to those who might not know him.

- *To whom could you show either respect or devotion today as Christ's ambassador?*

Talking It Out

1. During the time of Paul's writing of the letter to the Ephesians, wives were considered to be the property of their husbands, and in fact, it was perfectly legal for a man to beat his wife if he was unsatisfied with her. How does Paul's definition of marriage and its proper roles contradict these cultural norms? How does the Christian ideal of marriage elevate the roles of both husbands and wives?

2. Respect for those in authority, and for other people in general, seems to be slipping in our culture today. How can you show more love and respect to others? To those you know? To those placed in authority over you?

3. Does voluntary submission to one's spouse or to someone in authority mean that we should accept or allow abusive behavior to take place? Why or why not? If abuse is taking place in a Christian marriage or another relationship, what steps should be taken? Be sure to take into consideration what Paul said in Ephesians 4 and 5 about how we should live, especially with fellow believers.

LESSON 11

Practicing Loving Relationships

(6:1–9)

Our family relationships and our careers are two of the most important areas of life for most of us. The good news is that God is as concerned about our families, our children, our jobs, and our workplace relationships as we are. In Paul's letter to the Ephesians, he speaks to all of these relationships when he says, "Out of your reverence for Christ be supportive of each other in love" (Ephesians 5:21). Paul provides practical instruction for how we can live in Christ with those we encounter the most.

Parents and Children

Today's world can be perilous for our kids. It's easy to worry about their health, safety, education, and emotional well-being. But back in the ancient Roman world when Paul wrote the book of Ephesians, children faced even more perilous situations. Conditions were poor for many families, and unwanted children, especially if they were sick or born with deformities, were often cast off into the street or forest to fend for themselves. Children were second- or even third-class citizens, sold into slavery at times to pay off a family's debt. And in Roman society, fathers ruled their families with an iron fist. Their word in their households was as good as law, with little recourse for wives and children of abusive men. So Paul's words in Ephesians ran in direct opposition to the culture of his day. And they speak to us as well. God's plan is that our families be filled with love and peace.

- *Read Ephesians 6:1–4. Now think back to your family life when you were growing up. How did your childhood compare to the family dynamics that Paul describes in this passage?*

- *If you have children, have you ever "exasperated" them? In what ways could your parenting techniques be exasperating to your kids? What could you do differently to be a patient and loving example to your children while still training them up in obedience?*

- *Paul tells children that if they want to be "wise," they should "listen to their parents." Even if you do not have children or your parents have passed away or are no longer in your life, it is always a good thing to listen to the wise advice of our elders and mentors. Who has been a mentor in your walk with the Lord? How did his or her example help you gain the wisdom that you needed?*

- *What reason does Paul give for listening to wise parental guidance (vv. 2–3)?*

 # THE EXTRA MILE

Paul wants parents to replace approaches to child-rearing that routinely frustrate and anger children with the far better approach that uses biblical instruction and loving discipline (v. 4). If you're not sure what this includes or how to do this, you can find a good deal of help in the book of Proverbs. Studying and reflecting on this book's wise counsel and then putting it into practice in your own life as you implement it in your child-rearing will positively improve your family's dynamics and direction. Another source of insight can come from wise parents and grandparents, whether in your own extended family or your church family. Of course, you can find numerous articles, books, and online sources that offer beneficial guidance.

One more thing: your heavenly Father has provided you with the Holy Spirit who has come to "unveil the reality of every truth within [us]" (John 16:13). With humility and the hunger to know, regularly ask the Spirit to guide you in your parenting. Be open to his lead, including to those resources around you that he urges you to use and learn from. God wants to give you light, not leave you in darkness and confusion. Let him.

On the Job

Let's face it. If you are employed in a job or pursuing a career, you will spend most of your waking hours either working for an employer or striving to get ahead in a business or career path. What you do at the workplace matters to the Lord; he is concerned about every area of your life.

- *Read Ephesians 6:5–8. Paul tells us that when we are at our jobs, we should work for our employers as though they were Jesus himself. What is your relationship like with your boss or supervisor? (Or with your employees if you are the boss.)*

- *How might this relationship change if you began to "serve them with humility in your heart as though you were working for the Master"?*

- *It is easy to do the right thing when other people are watching you. What are some things people do at the office or on the job that are less than honest or fair when others might not be looking? Would your own behavior change if you continually remembered that the Holy Spirit within you is aware of what you are doing even if others are not?*

- *What is one practical way you could bless your employer or employees today?*

 EXPERIENCE GOD'S HEART

Throughout these verses, God's gracious love and assistance show through. When children are told to be obedient to their parents, Paul writes to them, "The Lord will help you" (v. 1). And when employers and employees are asked to treat each other with honor and respect, Paul reminds them: "Be assured that anything you do that is beautiful and excellent will be repaid by our Lord" (v. 8).

- *Has there ever been a time when God helped you as you wholeheartedly sought to honor him? Tell the story.*

- *We don't act in beautiful and excellent ways in order to gain payment from the Lord. Rather, we should do so out of the motivation of our love for him. But what a blessing it is that he promises to reward us! What rewards have you received from God for doing what was right?*

♥ SHARE GOD'S HEART

- *In Ephesians 6:9, Paul tells "caretakers of the flock"—leaders in the church and in the workplace—to "do what is right with your people," especially because God himself shows no favoritism. You may not be a church leader or a supervisor on the job, but of whom are you a caretaker? Whom do you influence on a day-to-day basis?*

- *How does this relationship reflect God's ideals? Do you "do what is right"? If not, how can you change?*

- *How can our practical behavior in our relationships with family members, with the people we work with, with those we see on a consistent basis demonstrate the love of God to others?*

- *Write out a prayer on a notecard, asking God to help you at your place of work and show you any areas where you need to improve or change your behavior to become more Christlike. Place it on the bathroom mirror or on the dashboard of your car and commit to praying it each morning before you begin your workday.*

- *It is believed that St. Francis of Assisi once declared, "Preach the gospel at all times. When necessary, use words." How can you preach the gospel to those around you this week—without using words?*

Talking It Out

1. No family is ever perfect, but some parents can be abusive to their children. How can children honor a mother or father who abuses them? To what extent do you believe this commandment should be followed?

2. Parents have many great responsibilities to their children: to provide a good home, an education, food, clothes, discipline, instruction, and so on. What is a believer's responsibility to his or her children? How are these responsibilities different from those of someone who doesn't know the Lord?

3. As representatives of God, we are to have a good work ethic and be exemplary employers and employees in the workplace. Read 1 Peter 2:18–21. What should you do if you have a disagreement with someone on the job? How are you to deal with a boss or supervisor you don't like? How does this behavior run counter to the culture in which we live?

LESSON 12

Spiritual Warfare

(6:10–24)

When you face conflict and challenges in your life, whom do you typically blame? Is it other people—maybe a difficult boss or coworker or perhaps a spouse or a child with whom you are having an argument? Or maybe your problems run deeper, into the realm of addiction or divorce or depression and anxiety. Paul concludes his letter to the Ephesians with words of hope. He even tells us that he has "saved these most important truths for last" (6:10). The good news is that the people and the problems we come up against in our lives are not the real problem. As Paul writes, "Your hand-to-hand combat is not with human beings, but with the highest principalities and authorities operating in rebellion under the heavenly realms" (v. 12).

The best news of all is that Jesus defeated the enemy, Satan, and all those he commands when he died on the cross (Colossians 2:13–15). They have been conquered by the reigning King, and while these enemies still operate in the earth today, we have authority over them as well. God has given us spiritual armor and weapons to protect us. With this armor and the Holy Spirit dwelling in us, we can stand strong against any attack the enemy tries to bring against us.

The Conflict

Believers within the body of Christ—in this case, the local church—compose the last group of relationships that Paul addresses with his directive to "be supportive of each other in love" (Ephesians 5:21). He wants us to understand that what lies behind the disorder, chaos, violence, corruption, and other indications of evil in this world are spiritual powers that are in rebellion against their Creator (6:12). He wants believers to unite against them, fighting spiritual enemies with the weapons he provides and protecting themselves with the equipment he supplies. When we do this, we lovingly support one another. United we stand; divided we fall (Mark 3:24–25).

- *When you encounter a conflict or challenge in your life, are you more likely to credit the devil or other human beings as the ultimate cause of the problem? Why? How can you strike a balance between the responsibility that people have for their own actions and the work of Satan and his demons in this world?*

- *What does it mean to be "supernaturally infused with strength through your life-union with the Lord Jesus" (Ephesians 6:10)?*

- *In what areas or situations do you need to "stand victorious with the force of his explosive power flowing in and through you" (v. 10)?*

Who's the Enemy?

One of the greatest strategies in warfare is to know as much as possible about the enemy before engaging him in battle. Paul's words in Ephesians 6 are like those of a general standing before his military troops, giving them a good description of who they are up against as well as a pep talk, reminding them that the victory is theirs. Our enemy is an "accuser" (v. 11), "operating in rebellion" and holding "this dark world in bondage" (v. 12), and a "slanderer" (v. 13). He and the principalities and powers that operate with him and beneath him are the ones we are actually struggling against.

Look up the following passages and jot down what you learn about Satan, our spiritual adversary.[35]

Luke 4:1–13

John 8:44

Ephesians 2:2

1 Peter 5:8–9

1 John 3:8, 10, 12

1 John 5:18–19

- *Has the enemy ever come against you in your mind, accusing you or slandering you by bringing up faults, imperfections, or past sins? If so, remember what 1 John 1:9 declares: God is faithful to forgive you when you come to him in repentance! Write a brief prayer of thankfulness to the Father for his forgiveness, which leaves you free of any accusation by the enemy.*

- *Have you ever underestimated the power of the devil in this world? In your own life? Have you ever overestimated his power? Tell the story.*

The Belt of Truth

After Paul describes the true enemy that we face, he describes the "complete set of armor" that God has provided so that we can stand victorious against any attacks Satan may launch against us. Again, this armor is complete—it is all we will ever need *if* we apply it to our lives.

In the days of the Roman empire, a soldier who was going into battle would tuck his garment up into his belt when he needed his legs free to run quickly or dodge oncoming weapons. The belt also held various other pieces of armor (such as the shield) and a sheath for the soldier's sword. Paul tells us to "Put on truth as a belt to strengthen you to stand in triumph" (Ephesians 6:14). Just as the belt of a Roman soldier held together the other pieces of armor and held his garments in place, so our "belt of truth" is foundational to our ability to stand against the lies and deceptions of the devil.

Read the following passages and write down the sources of truth they mention.[36]

John 14:6

John 17:17

Romans 1:19–20

Romans 2:2

Romans 2:14–15

Based on what you discovered, answer these questions:

Does Scripture indicate that we can know truth?

Are we responsible for the truth we know?

Who is the ultimate Knower?

- *What are some practical steps you can take to learn more of God's truth?*

- *What are some truths you already know that you can use to combat the evil one?*

Holiness That Covers Your Heart

Roman soldiers wore a breastplate, a piece of armor that covered them from the neck to their thighs, protecting their vital organs from penetration by the weapons of their enemies. It would have been unthinkable to go into battle without this important piece of armor. They would have been dead men walking! Paul calls "holiness" the protection that we have that covers our hearts (Ephesians 6:14).

According to Bible scholar Merrill F. Unger, "Holiness is a general term used [in Scripture] to indicate sanctity or separation from all that is sinful, impure, or morally imperfect." Put positively, holiness is "moral wholeness."[37]

- *How could failing to strive for true holiness make a person be vulnerable to attacks by the enemy?*

- *In what areas of your life do you fall short of moral wholeness?*

• *Remember 1 John 1:9 and bring those areas to the Lord.*
Ask for forgiveness and for the help of the Holy Spirit
within you to overcome the sin that still lingers in your life.

Standing Alert on Your Feet

In addition to their breastplates, Roman soldiers typically wore soft leather sandals with studs on the soles, like cleats, to hold them steady, especially when they were fighting in hand-to-hand combat. These sandals were sturdy enough for one-on-one fighting but also light enough to allow soldiers to cross great distances in a short period of time. As we stand steady in warfare against the enemy, we must also be ready to stand our ground and share the "blessings of peace" with those around us (Ephesians 6:15).

• *How could establishing peace with other human beings*
defeat the plans of Satan?

- *What "blessings" has peace—peace with God, peace with other people—brought into your life?*

- *Who in your life needs the blessing of peace? How can you share it with them?*

The Wrap-Around Shield of Faith

Paul writes that faith works as a shield for us in every battle, wrapping around us to "extinguish the blazing arrows coming at [us] from the evil one!" (v. 16).

- *What are some "blazing arrows" that the devil flings at you?*

- *How does your faith extinguish them?*

- *What can you do to bring about a greater level of faith in your life?*

The Helmet of Salvation's Full Deliverance

The helmet of a Roman soldier was the next-to-last piece of armor he would place on his body in preparation for battle. Its purpose was to protect his head from the blows of swords and arrows flung at him from his enemies. For Paul, one of the ways salvation's helmet protects us is against Satan's lies (vv. 17–18).

- *What are some satanically influenced lies that seek to undermine the confidence of believers in their standing before God as saved by Christ?*

- *Have you seen some of the consequences of these lies in the lives of people you know? In your own life? What damages have they brought about?*

- *What truths can you use to counter these lies?*

The Razor-Sharp Spirit-Sword

The sword was the primary offensive weapon of the Roman soldier, but for followers of Jesus, the sword we use to attack and defeat the enemy is the Word of God, illuminated by the Holy Spirit who inspired those words in the first place.

- *Read Matthew 4:1–11. How did Jesus use the Spirit-sword in his own stand against the devil?*

- *If you have not read God's Word or spent time studying it, you won't be prepared when Satan's attacks come against you or those around you. How can you grow in your knowledge and application of the Bible?*[38]

- *What battles are you currently facing in your spiritual life? What are some Scripture verses or passages that apply to your situation? Commit to the memorization of a few of them to build your faith and help you in your stand against the enemy.*

Prayer and Blessing

Paul concludes his letter with a call for believers to "pray passionately in the Spirit, as you constantly intercede with every form of prayer at all times. Pray the blessings of God upon all his believers" (Ephesians 6:18). And he adds a request that they pray for him and his ministry to "preach the wonderful mystery of the hope-filled gospel" and that he do so "with bold freedom at every opportunity" (vv. 19–20).

- *Although Paul doesn't explicitly connect his exhortation to pray and the armor of God theme, it's not difficult to see how prayer can be an effective spiritual weapon in the conflict with Satan. When we pray for one another in the body of Christ, we call on God to intercede in the lives of his forever family members. Take some time now to pray for specific believers and make this a regular habit in your life. The church needs prayer warriors.*

- *While Paul's calling was to present and defend the gospel, the good news about Jesus Christ, all of us, whether evangelists or not, are urged to share the gospel with others. How have you done that in your life?*

- *What are some ways of sharing the gospel that you have found especially effective? Remember, effectiveness does not always equate with all hearers becoming Christians. Not even Paul could bring that about through his efforts (Acts 14:1–4; 17:1–4, 32–34). Sharing the gospel can simply be a time where you make the message clearer or answer an objection to it or soften someone's heart toward the good news.*[39]

 EXPERIENCE GOD'S HEART

- *When you pray, do you do so out of a habit or a ritual? Or do you "pray passionately in the Spirit" (Ephesians 6:18)? How can you invite into your prayer life more of the Holy Spirit and his passion for you, for those you know, and for the world?*

- *What are the specific requests Paul says we should pray for in verses 19–20?*

- *When was the last time you prayed for these requests? Commit to praying more for God's revelation and his gospel to be spread throughout the world.*

 SHARE GOD'S HEART

- *What are some of the blessings Paul speaks over his readers in verses 21–23?*

- *Who in your life needs to know more about the passionate God, the One who longs to "shower his peace" and "fill our hearts" with "the blessings of faith and love" and "abundant grace"? How can you share these truths that you have learned in this study with them?*

Paul's Benediction

Paul sent his letter to the Ephesian believers through a messenger named Tychicus. Paul described Tychicus as a "dear friend," a "beloved brother," and a "trustworthy minister" (vv. 21–22). In addition to delivering the written correspondence, Tychicus would share all of Paul's concerns for the Ephesians and let them know how the apostle was doing. And he would also prophesy over the people to encourage their hearts.

- *We don't hear much in the Scriptures about Tychicus, but clearly, he was an important person in Paul's life and a crucial member of the early church. Do you know any "unsung heroes" of the faith today? Who are they, and what work do they accomplish behind the scenes?*

- *When you volunteer to help in church activities or to perform some task on behalf of the Lord or his church, how important is it to you to receive recognition? What can you do this week to help someone else—without receiving any credit?*

- *Paul wrote a magnificent benediction in his letter to the church at Ephesus. Read 6:23–24 aloud, substituting your own name for the word "you" in the passage. What stood out to you as you read these words? Did they draw you closer to the Lord? If so, how?*

Talking It Out

1. When you experience difficulties or "attacks" in the form of temptation, everyday problems, or conflict in your relationships, which parts of the armor of God are the strongest for you? Which are the weakest in your life? How could you strengthen each piece of the armor in your arsenal?

2. The command to "pray passionately in the Spirit" follows directly after Paul's discussion of each piece of the divine armor. Why do you think this command is given in this context? How does praying in the Spirit help you in times when Satan is attacking?

3. Paul's final prayer requests in Ephesians relate to the spread of the gospel throughout the world. Where do such requests usually fall on your list of priorities in your times of prayer? How can you make it a greater priority?

4. Consider the time you have spent digging into the book of Ephesians in this study. What personal applications will you take away that will make a permanent and practical change in your life? How will this affect your relationship with God? Your relationships with other people?

Endnotes

1   "About The Passion Translation," *The Passion Translation: The New Testament with Psalms, Proverbs, and Song of Songs* (Savage, MN: BroadStreet Publishing Group, 2017), iv.

2   Brian Simmons, "Ephesians: Introduction," *The Passion Translation* (Savage, MN: BroadStreet Publishing, 2020), 527.

3   Lesley Adkins and Roy A. Adkins, *Handbook to Life in Ancient Rome* (New York: Oxford University Press, 1994), 38–47; W. G. Hardy, *The Greek and Roman World*, revised ed. (Cambridge, MA: Schenkman Publishing Co., 1970), 73–78.

4   F. F. Bruce, *Jesus and Paul: Places They Knew* (Nashville, TN: Thomas Nelson, 1981), 125.

5   Hardy, *The Greek and Roman World*, 80.

6   Bruce, *Jesus and Paul*, 106.

7   Richard L. Niswonger, *New Testament History* (Grand Rapids, MI: Zondervan, 1988), 231.

8   E. M. Blaiklock, "Ephesus," *The Zondervan Pictorial Encyclopedia of the Bible*, 5 vols. (Grand Rapids, MI: Zondervan, 1976), vol. 2, 328.

9   Bruce, *Jesus and Paul*, 109.

10   *Encyclopaedia Britannica*, s.v. "Ephesus," accessed April 8, 2021, https://www.britannica.com/place/Ephesus.

11   "Map of the Roman Empire—Ephesus," *Bible History*, accessed April 8, 2021, https://www.bible-history.com/maps/romanempire/Ephesus.html.

12   Jay Rambo, "The Task of the Church #1," Sermoncentral.com, October 16, 2001, www.sermoncentral.com/sermons/the-task-of-the-church-1-jay-rambo-sermon-on-church-purpose-of-40072.

13   Lawrence O. Richards, "Apostle," *Expository Dictionary of Bible Words* (Grand Rapids, MI: Zondervan Publishing House, 1985), 59.

14   Richards, "Predestine," *Expository Dictionary of Bible Words*, 501–502.

15   If you would like to explore this theological mystery further, here are some helpful resources: *Predestination and Free Will: Four Views of Divine Sovereignty and Human Freedom*, eds. David Basinger and Randall Basinger (Downers Grove, IL: InterVarsity Press, 1986); Alan P. F. Sell, *The Great Debate: Calvinism, Arminianism, and Salvation*, reprint ed. (Grand Rapids, MI: Baker Book House, 1983); Norman L. Geisler, *Chosen But Free: A Balanced View of God's Sovereignty and Free Will*, 3rd ed. (Minneapolis, MN: Bethany House, 2010), and "Freedom, Free Will, and Determinism," *Evangelical Dictionary of Theology*, ed. Walter A. Elwell (Grand Rapids, MI: Baker Book House, 1984), 428–30; Robert Shank, *Elect in the Son: A Study of the Doctrine of Election*, reprint ed. (Minneapolis, MN: Bethany House, 1989); Roger T. Forster and V. Paul Marston, *God's Strategy in Human History*, 2nd ed. (Eugene, OR: Wipf and Stock, 2000); William Lane Craig, *The Only Wise God: The Compatibility of Divine Foreknowledge and Human Freedom*, reprint ed. (Eugene, OR: Wipf and Stock, 1999).

16   Charles Hodge, cited in *Search the Scriptures*, ed. Alex M. Stibbs (Downers Grove, IL: InterVarsity Press, 1979), 218.

17   William Barclay, *The Letter to the Galatians and Ephesians* (Philadelphia: Westminster, 1976), 80.

18   Joyce Meyer, *Ephesians: A Biblical Study* (New York: FaithWords, 2020), 26–27.

19   James Strong, "dunameos," *The New Strong's Expanded Exhaustive Concordance of the Bible* (Nashville, TN: Thomas Nelson, 2010).

20   Strong, "energeian," *The New Strong's Expanded Exhaustive Concordance of the Bible*.

21   Strong, "kratous," *The New Strong's Expanded Exhaustive Concordance of the Bible*.

22   Strong, "ischuos," *The New Strong's Expanded Exhaustive Concordance of the Bible*.

23   Clinton E. Arnold, "Magic," *Dictionary of Paul and His Letters*, ed. Gerald F. Hawthorne, Ralph P. Martin, and Daniel G. Reid (Downers Grove, IL: InterVarsity Press, 1993), 580–81.

24   Daniel G. Reid, "Principalities and Powers," *Dictionary of Paul and His Letters*, 749.

25   Henri Blocher, *In the Beginning: The Opening Chapters of Genesis* (Downers Grove, IL: InterVaristy Press, 1984), 171–72.

26   Augustine, *Seven Questions Concerning the Heptateuch*, 2.73.

27   Elizabeth George, *Ephesians: Understanding Your Blessings in Christ* (Eugene, OR: Harvest House, 2008), 66.

28   H. A. Ironside, *Ephesians: An Ironside Expository Commentary* (Grand Rapids, MI: Kregel, 1937; reprint 2007), 107.

29   David C. George, *2 Corinthians, Galatians, Ephesians*, Layman's Bible Book Commentary, 24 vols. (Nashville, TN: Broadman Press, 1979), vol. 21, 119.

30   Meyer, *Ephesians*, 105–106.

31   Ephesians 4:17, note 'a,' TPT.

32   Will Norton Jr., "Conversations: Why John Grisham Teaches Sunday School," *Christianity Today*, October 3, 1994, https://www.christianitytoday.com/ct/1994/october3/4tb014.html.

33   Manfred T. Brauch, *Hard Sayings of Paul* (Downers Grove, IL: InterVarsity Press, 1989), 215.

34   Brauch, *Hard Sayings of Paul*, 216.

35   To learn even more about our adversary, the devil, and the demons who serve him, see C. Fred Dickason, *Angels, Elect and Evil* (Chicago: Moody Press, 1975), part 2.

36   The subject of the nature and sources of truth and how we can know it is a complex one. Some excellent Christian discussions of this subject can be found in these resources: Harry Blamires, *The Christian Mind: How Should a Christian Think?* (Ann Arbor, MI: Servant Books, 1978); J. Budziszewski, *What We Can't Not Know: A Guide* (Dallas, TX: Spence Publishing Co., 2003), and *Written on the Heart: The Case for Natural Law* (Downers Grove, IL: InterVarsity Press, 1997); Bradley G. Green, *The Gospel and the Mind: Recovering and Shaping the Intellectual Life* (Wheaton, IL: Crossway, 2010); Norman L. Geisler, "Truth, Nature of," in *Baker Encyclopedia of Christian Apologetics* (Grand Rapids, MI: Baker Books, 1999), 741–45; Vernon C. Grounds, "The Truth about Truth," in *Journal of the Evangelical Theological Society* 38:2 (June 1995), 219–29; Arthur F. Holmes, *All Truth Is God's Truth* (Downers Grove, IL: InterVarsity Press, 1977); and J. P. Moreland, *Love Your God with All Your Mind: The Role of Reason in the Life of the Soul* (Colorado Springs, CO: NavPress, 1997).

37   Merrill F. Unger, "Holiness," *The New Unger's Bible Dictionary*, ed. R. K. Harrison (Chicago, IL: Moody Press, 1988), 581.

38 Two online sources that offer worthwhile Bible study help are biblegateway.com and biblehub.com. Two excellent books are: Gordon D. Fee and Douglas Stuart, *How to Read the Bible for All Its Worth*, 4th ed. (Grand Rapids, MI: Zondervan, 2014); and Howard G. Hendricks and William D. Hendricks, *Living by the Book: The Art and Science of Reading the Bible*, revised ed. (Chicago: Moody Press, 2007).

39 Here are some insightful and helpful resources on sharing the gospel: David Geisler and Norman Geisler, *Conversational Evangelism* (Eugene, OR: Harvest House, 2014); Gregory Koukl, *Tactics: A Game Plan for Discussing Your Christian Convictions*, revised ed. (Grand Rapids, MI: Zondervan, 2019); Rebecca Manley Pippert, *Out of the Saltshaker and into the World: Evangelism as a Way of Life*, 2nd ed. (Downers Grove, IL: InterVarsity Press, 1999). When it comes to answering challenges to the Christian faith, among the many excellent resources are these: Norman L. Geisler and Ronald M. Brooks, *When Skeptics Ask: A Handbook on Christian Evidences* (Grand Rapids, MI: Baker Books, 2013); Fred von Kamecke, *Busted: Exposing Popular Myths about Christianity* (Grand Rapids, MI: Zondervan, 2009); Lee Strobel, *The Case for Faith: A Journalist Investigates the Toughest Objections to Christianity* (Grand Rapids, MI: Zondervan, 2014). Some helpful online resources are: str.org (Stand to Reason); josh.org (Josh McDowell Ministry); ngim.org (Norm Geisler International Ministries); discovery.org (Discovery Institute).